Inner Adventures

Cover art by *Jane A. Evans*

INNER ADVENTURES

Thought, Intuition and Beyond

E. LESTER SMITH

*This publication made possible with
the assistance of the Kern Foundation*

A Quest Book

The Theosophical Publishing House
Wheaton, Ill. U.S.A.
Madras, India / London, England

The Theosophical Publishing House
306 West Geneva Road
Wheaton, IL 60187
A publication of the Theosophical Publishing House, a department of the Theosophical Society in America.

Library of Congress Cataloging-in-Publication Data

Smith, E. Lester (Ernest Lester), 1904-
  Inner adventures.
  "A Quest original"—T.p. verso.
  Bibliography: p.
  Includes index.
  1. Thought and thinking. 2. Consciousness.
3. Mind-brain identity theory. I. Title.
BF441.S63   1988   153   87-40520
ISBN 0-8356-0627-9 (pbk.)

Printed in the United States of America

To my Winifred, who for five years
patiently endured my compulsive urge
to get this book written

Only let me say this, that to my mind there is a great field of science which is as yet quite closed to us. I refer to the science which proceeds in terms of life and is established on data of living experience and of sure intuition. Call it subjective science if you like. Our objective science of modern knowledge concerns itself only with phenomena, and with phenomena as regarded in their cause-and-effect relationship. I have nothing to say against such science. It is perfect as far as it goes. But to regard it as exhausting the whole scope of human possibility in knowledge seems to me just puerile. Our science is a science of the dead world. Even biology never considers life, but only mechanistic functioning and apparatus of life.

D.H. Lawrence

Contents

x   **Contents**

Preface

The inspiration to write this book came from three main sources: first, lectures and books by Sir John Eccles and his collaborators, Sir Karl Popper and Prof. D. N. Robinson; second, lectures and books by the late Edward Gardner and personal friendship with him and a group of associates; third, books by Prof. Michael Whiteman and personal friendship nourished mainly by extensive correspondence over a number of years. He also read a draft of the book and gave many helpful suggestions towards its revision, especially of Chapters 11 and 16. Thanks are also due to Shirley Nicholson and some of her colleagues who read drafts of a few early chapters and offered advice and encouragement to complete the project. Early notes were discussed with a group of colleagues, to whom I also offer my thanks. My wife also deserves grateful appreciation for her patient support and forbearance. Some of the material was used originally in lectures or articles, but has been greatly revised for the book.

Over the several years that it took to write and rewrite, the book seemed to take on a life of its own; it has come out very differently from what I originally envisaged. In the course of the work, I have learned a great deal myself; I no longer seem to be the same man who initiated the project. One thing I have learned is that both nature and life are exceedingly complex. Neither can be constrained within relatively simple hypotheses or theories; these explain only part of the truth, and often another part of it remains in the hypothesis discarded in favor of the new one. But the whole truth lies beyond any mental processes and can only be apprehended in mystical understanding. However, this is only accessible, save sporadically, to those who have made considerable progress in spiritual living. It is reluctance to embrace this quest that nourishes materialism and reductionism.

Each chapter is in a sense an independent essay on some facet of the overall theme. The order of the chapters has been changed several times. As now arranged, the scientific and philosophical chapters lead up to the last three, which might be regarded as a brief guide to the spiritual life, though no such presumption figured in my original intentions.

1

How We Think

*Radical materialism . . . must be an embarrassing belief
to acknowledge publicly when it is recognized as negat-
ing even one's own conscious belief and experiences!
Radical materialism should have a prominent place in
the history of human silliness.*

Sir John Eccles

How do we think? For the materialist and reductionist
there is no problem. He believes that he thinks with his
brain alone; he does not accept the existence of any nonphysical entity called mind. If he uses the word "mind"
at all, it is to signify merely the brain along with its
workings (Gilling and Brightwell 1962; A. Smith 1984).*
But for the large proportion of thinking people who
know from their own experience that there is more to
human life than the physical body and visible environment, there *is* a problem. They use the term "mind" to
signify (often in a rather loosely defined fashion) some
part of their own nonphysical psyche that is concerned
with thinking and that is superior to and the director
of the physical brain. It is in this sense that "mind" is
used in this book, and the main purpose of the book is
to clarify the complex situation.

*Masculine pronouns like he, him, his are used for convenience only and
are intended to include women as well.

So do we think with the brain alone, or with the mind alone, or with the brain and the mind working together? Since thinking is the most characteristically human of all our activities and arguably the most interesting, we really ought to know the answers to these questions. There are indeed many people who are certain that they *do* know, but others strongly disagree with them. If we accept that the questions remain open, how can we resolve them? Where can we find information on all aspects of the controversy? How do we set about the exciting task of thinking about thinking?

These are the problems to which this book addresses itself. We shall come to the conclusions that the brain can indeed think on its own, after its fashion, and can put up a highly creditable performance. The mind too can think alone, after its distinctly different fashion. But usually mind and brain work together in an almost unbelievably intimate and fruitful partnership. Out of this partnership come all the awe-inspiring achievements of humanity to date which permit us to take a supremely optimistic view of human potential still to be realized. The quest will take us into rarely plumbed depths and heights of the human psyche. It is doubtful if the mind can ever know itself fully. Awareness of the workings of the mind surely calls for a capability *beyond the mind*. In the finality, it becomes a quest by the human spirit that each must undertake for himself. But there is a lot of exploring to be done before that final stage is reached.

Information and ideas on modes of thinking, or the mind-brain problem, can be found in three broad areas of study. First comes research on the brain, the province of anatomy, neurophysiology, biochemistry, and surgery. Second comes research on the mind, the province of psychology and psychiatry. Finally comes philosophy, both Western and Eastern, including understanding gained by introspection and yogic meditation. These three sources give independent and largely unrelated accounts of the situation. Attempts have been made to correlate these accounts in pairs, but few if any of the available books attempt to combine information from all three sources into an overall picture. This book does essay the daunting task, in the manner of a preliminary enquiry, for general readers. It is not highly technical; references are illustrative rather than exhaustive. It does not pretend to provide definitive answers, but rather to stimulate further thinking. It is frankly speculative in places.

Many people engaged in brain research simply ignore the mind. Others face the issue and argue forcefully that what is called mind has no existence apart from the brain and that thinking is a function of the brain alone. This materialistic stance is taken in all sincerity by eminent scientists, Nobel laureates among them. It has been presented at length on British television and radio by Colin Blakemore among others, and is argued cogently in a book based on the television series (Gilling and Brightwell 1962). It is the orthodox view still taught in universities. A recent exposition in this manner is the book *The Mind* by Anthony Smith, which follows on his earlier book *The Body*. The author does not believe in a nonmaterial mind. He uses the word—very sparingly— simply as a semantic convenience, an omnibus word for the brain plus its activities. The book is in fact an excellent popular account of the anatomy, biochemistry, and physiology of the brain, and of how it operates in receiving information from the sense organs and initiating appropriate responses. It appears to offer complete and adequate explanations on this totally materialistic basis—until one reflects upon what is omitted.

Most neurophysiologists started out with the nineteenth-century idea that "the brain secretes thought as the liver secretes bile." But some of them have been

driven by the results of their own researches to accept
the concept of an immaterial mind using the physical
brain as its instrument. In contrast, many psychologists
simply take the mind for granted. They refer all thinking to the mind and tend to ignore the brain as if it
played no significant part in thought processes. Cognitive psychologists recognize both, but refuse to attempt
any discrimination between them; they relegate both
to a "black box," the lid of which it would be improper
to lift, and refer all thinking to an indivisible mind-brain
complex. Psychologists in general seem to expend a lot
of time and energy on "proving" what is blindingly obvious to any perceptive person; or alternatively in
reaching dubious conclusions through the self-imposed
restrictions of their approach. They feel obliged to use
rigid scientific methodology that is not suited to their
subject.

BRAIN, MIND, AND SELF

A dualistic position, recognizing both mind and brain,
is strongly championed by Sir Karl Popper and Sir John
Eccles in their book *The Self and its Brain* (Popper and
Eccles 1977). Collaboration between Popper, the cele-
brated philosopher, and Eccles, the neurophysiologist
and Nobel laureate, proved highly fruitful. It may be
noted, however, that this brain-mind dualism is not the
classical dualism between ultimate opposites like spirit
and matter, good and evil (see Chapter 13). Instead, it
contrasts two closely related aspects of a single system,
the thinking process. It resembles the more fundamental dualities only in that one component is material, the
other nonmaterial; so it does pose similar philosophic
difficulties.

Philosophers acquire their ideas by cogitation and introspection. Most of us pay respectful attention to what

they say, which implies that we accept their techniques as valid. However, the validity of introspection as a means to examine the mind has been questioned, so it is important to resolve this crucial issue. Anthony Smith (Smith 1984) says "we have only our brain to puzzle out our mind." If this were indeed so, the prospect of success would be small. In *The Self and its Brain* (Popper and Eccles 1977), Popper faces up to this problem of how the mind can monitor its own activities. He rejects the solution that the mind can be divided into a "lower" and a "higher" portion, such that the latter can observe the activities of the former. Instead he comes up with the ingenious solution that the mind does not actually monitor what it is thinking in the present, but what it *was* thinking in the immediate past. Naturally the mind can do this. However, it is not introspection but merely memory recall. Introspection, as generally understood, is being aware of the mind's activities *in real time* at the immediate moment of their occurrence. Anyone who has his mind under reasonable control can verify this for himself. So how can this undoubtedly real phenomenon be explained? It can only be done by postulating some part of ourselves that is superior to the mind. It necessitates a tripartite division into self, mind, and brain. This state of affairs is implicit in the book cited, since its title includes two of these components, and mind is repeatedly mentioned in the text. It is implicit too in some of the diagrams in the second part of the book. But Eccles does not develop the theme to any degree.

Since I can ask myself the question, "What is my mind thinking about?" it is clear that we commonly recognize a distinction between the self (the I) and the mind, which is *used* for thinking. Then if the thoughts are to be put into words and perhaps written down, we recognize that a third entity becomes involved, namely the brain. So this triple division derives not from some abstruse philosophy, but from common knowledge. We know these things already "in the back of the mind," as we say. If we bring them "to the front of the mind" and set them down in words, we recognize their truth.

If we decide to take up meditation, then the first lesson is concentration or mind control. The mind must be restrained from idle wandering, and must be brought to bear wholly upon the object of the exercise. But this is common practice among creative thinkers. Interest in what they are doing, scientific research perhaps or composing music, impels them to concentrate fully on the work in hand. So what is it that provides the impulse? It must be something *other than* the mind, something that regards the mind as its servant. It is the "I," our very self. In its turn, the mind regards the brain as its servant. Thus is established once again the postulated threefold division. Some people, however, refuse to accept this obvious conclusion because they have been preconditioned by the doctrines of radical materialism and reductionism. I regard these as false and cowardly doctrines. They survive, I suggest, because in effect they absolve us from moral responsibility by asserting that everything is determined by purely material causes. This is a comforting and self-indulgent creed. It takes courage to reject this implied immunity and to accept full responsibility for all our actions. The odd thing is that philosophers who propound these materialistic ideas do not themselves behave in this irresponsible fashion. In other words, they act as if they do not really believe what they proclaim. Unfortunately, it is their less intelligent followers who take their words literally and make of them an excuse for wrongdoing.

Since the validity of introspection is fairly generally accepted in Western philosophy, it is surprising that relatively few people are prepared to accept what has been said by Eastern philosophers, some of it thousands of years ago. Yet these men perfected and extended their techniques of cogitation and introspection through half a lifetime or more of yoga practices, including guided meditation. Thus they gained understanding of realms of being and states of consciousness far beyond anything generally recognized in the Western world. A supreme example is the *Yoga Sutras of Patanjali*. This work was presumably written as an *aide-memoire* to verbal instruction. It is so concise and condensed that it is almost useless without an extensive commentary. One of the most authoritative is that by I. K. Taimni (1975).

With our arrogant pride in modern experimental science, we find it too humiliating to accept that these ancient seers got there first, in some respects. But they also recognized that the wisdom they gained could not be passed on effectively by discourses or books. These can do little more than inspire others to follow the same road. There are a few in the West who have done just that. Among them are those who have expressed what they have discovered in modern language, easier to follow than the ancient Eastern writings, which are available to Western readers mostly in inadequate translations from Sanskrit or other oriental languages, understood by few Westerners. Some of the later authors have also been able to correlate their understanding with modern scientific theories, in physics especially. This provides, so to speak, a dual verification: on the one hand it testifies to the truth of the spiritual messages of yogis and mystics, and on the other to the validity in general terms of quantum physics and other related ideas.

Not surprisingly, these sources have little to say about the brain. They are nevertheless valuable to this project because they integrate mind into a wider spectrum of states of consciousness than is generally recognized in the West; they are also helpful in relation to the nature of memory.

RÉSUMÉ

The word "mind" has two quite different connotations. To the materialist and reductionist, it signifies merely the brain plus its functioning. To the many people who recognize nonmaterial components of the human psyche, "mind" signifies a superphysical entity that directs and uses the physical brain. Information about the thinking system derives from three main sources: research on the brain; research on the mind; and introspection and philosophy, both Western and Eastern. This book aims to correlate all three. Our ability to think about thinking necessitates not just two but three components, brain, mind, and self. This conclusion derives from common knowledge, rather than abstruse philosophy, but it can be illuminated, particularly by oriental philosophy.

2

The Brain:
Anatomy and Functions

Great advances have been made in understanding the working of the nervous system, and we have even a rough idea how that most subtle and elaborate of all computers, the human brain, performs its functions. The conception of molecular codes and the chemical storage of information which have arisen from work on reproduction have stimulated fascinating speculations about the mechanism of memory and even about the ancient mystery of dreams.

But what remains utterly incomprehensible is how and why the brain becomes the vehicle of consciousness. . . . Some philosophers have wanted to talk away the mind-matter problem as a mere verbal confusion. I suspect that at bottom they simply attach no importance to the scientific description of things and are therefore indifferent to any divorce between it and the language which describes the world of conscious experience. If so, they are of course entitled to remain indifferent; but men of science presumably do not.

Sir Cyril Hinshelwood

The human brain is the most wonderful object in the entire universe. It is the most complex and multifunctional of all organs. The simplest way to describe its elaborate three-dimensional organization is probably to start at the bottom and back, where the brain joins the spinal cord, and proceed stepwise to the top and front. This sequence is also logical since it follows roughly the evolutionary development.

We meet first the ancient reptilian brain and the mammalian brain, though these have in part been assigned new functions to meet human needs. For example, the sense of smell is far more important to animals than to us; they needed a larger proportion of the brain to process and distinguish odor impressions. In human brains most of the olfactory region is put to other uses. Nevertheless, we have more of it left than most of us use. The olfactory sense can be cultivated greatly, and this is done, for example, by some chemists and by wine-tasters and especially by blenders of perfumes. As our needs expanded, newer parts of the brain developed, increased in size, and became crowded into a skull already as large as is anatomically convenient.

The brain is subdivided in various ways to assist description, but the naming is somewhat confused. Both Latin and Greek roots have been used, while some areas are named after their discoverers. We may start with a simple three-part division into 1) hindbrain; 2) midbrain; and 3) forebrain or cerebrum. The hindbrain and midbrain together occupy about ⅙ of the total volume, while the forebrain occupies the remaining ⅚.

Subdivisions of the Brain

The hindbrain (or rhombencephalon, containing the cerebellum and medulla oblongata) is mainly concerned with bodily movement. Linking hindbrain to midbrain is the Pons Variolus. The midbrain (or mesencephalon), which is hardly an inch across, is concerned with responses to light and sound and also with sleep. The hindbrain and midbrain jointly are called the brain stem or the old (animal) brain. It is these parts of the brain that enable us to perform habitual movements and learned skills without conscious thought, such as cycling, swimming, and typing.

Linking midbrain to forebrain is the diencephalon. This contains regions of great functional importance: the thalamus, a sort of exchange junction through which pass nearly all the nerve impulses from the brain; the epithalamus, a small region that includes the pineal gland; the subthalamus; and finally the hypothalamus, very small but vital, since it is the main controller of the autonomic nervous system, and is also concerned with temperature regulation and with emotions. (See Figure 1).

The forebrain (prosencephalon or cerebrum) is by far

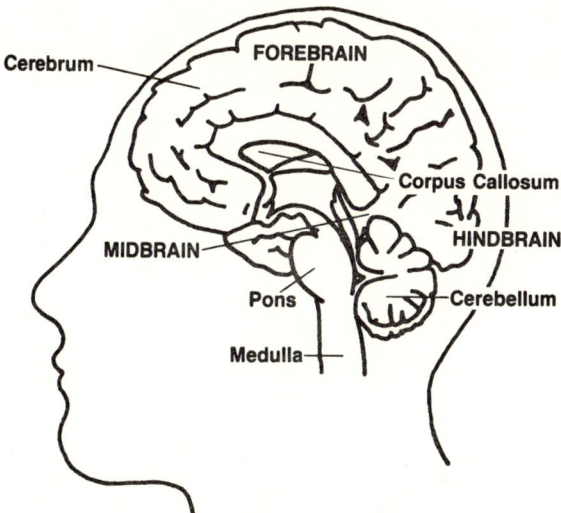

Fig. 1. Cross Section of the brain within the skull. The hindbrain and midbrain together form the brain stem. The cerebellum and medulla are in the hindbrain. The forebrain or cerebrum is divided into two hemispheres connected by the corpus callosum.

the largest region of the human brain. It is divided into eight parts. The primary division is into the two cerebral hemispheres, the "left brain" and "right brain" as they are popularly called (Figure 2). Although physically almost completely separate and with distinct functions (see Chapter 7), they are intimately linked by the corpus callosum, a thick cable of nerve fibers through which they intercommunicate. Thus their functions are fully integrated in the normal brain; only when the corpus callosum is severed, in a desperate bid to control epilepsy, can the separate functions of the two hemispheres be studied in detail (Figure 3).

Each hemisphere is in turn subdivided into four parts: 1) frontal lobes behind the forehead, concerned with intellect and planning; 2) parietal lobes at the top rear of the head, the sensory and motor areas; 3) temporal lobes, below and central, concerned with memory and emotions; and 4) occipital lobes, below at the rear,

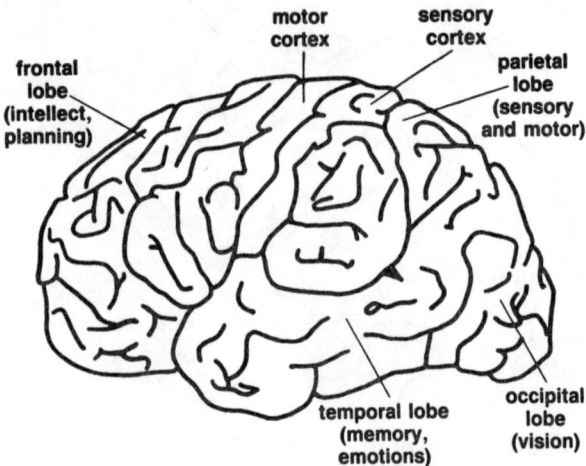

Fig. 2. The left hemisphere of the brain. Each hemisphere is divided into four lobes, the frontal, parietal, occipital, and temporal. The lobes have specialized functions.

Fig. 3. A split-brain patient drawing with both hands. Information from the left visual field is passed to the right brain, which controls the left hand. Thus the patient is able to copy the tree only with his left hand, not his right, since the left brain is unaware of information in the right brain. The patient's right hand can copy only the flower, not the tree.

which include the visual regions. The endbrain and basal ganglia are also within the cerebrum.

Finally the whole brain is wrapped in a tough membrane, the menenges, and is supported, like a jelly in a mold, within the skull. Curiously, the menenges is the only part of the brain that experiences pain when it is cut or otherwise injured. But the brain does of course respond with the sensation of pain to injuries to other parts of the body; moreover it can generate internal pain—headache and migraine for example.

In some respects the most important part of both hemispheres is the outer layer, the cerebral cortex, with its six distinct layers of cells. This may be likened to a television screen, or more closely to the visual display unit of a computer. On the "screen" is displayed all the information garnered by the sense organs, for appraisal by the conscious mind. But it is a two-way interface; the mind can initiate action in response to the information displayed.

Pursuing the computer analogy a little further, it is as though the thinker could manipulate the keyboard, to call up memories and to request further information from the senses. He can then command the body to do whatever is appropriate. But the analogy must not be taken too far. The mind-brain-body relationship is far more intimate than any such mechanism suggests. Moreover, it is so familiar and commonplace that analysis is difficult, especially for the materialist. It becomes meaningful only when we recognize ourselves as nonmaterial, spiritual beings, equipped with a material body and brain.

The miracle-like feature of this assembly is the cerebral cortex through which interaction between the two realms can occur. Some scientists have faced this situation and have nevertheless remained materialists. Others have found it impossible to maintain this stance, and yet others have wavered. For example Anthony Smith, whose only use for the word "mind" is to signify the brain plus its functions, wrote concerning the evolution of the brain: "There is such a logic to the story that it does seem preordained, like evolution with a purpose, the destination destined from the very start."

Nervous System: Brain Biochemistry

This chapter is intended to outline only the gross divisions of the brain. The operation of the cerebral cortex will be detailed in Chapter 6. But at this point it is necessary to say something about nerves and the nervous system and about brain biochemistry.

The brain is extremely active in its metabolism. Although its weight is only about 2 percent of the total body weight, it consumes about 20 percent of the oxygen and glucose available in the circulating blood; that is to say, it works ten times as fast as the rest of the body. Deprivation of oxygen for only four minutes can cause irreparable brain damage. In electrical terms, the brain consumes about 20 watts of energy continuously—enough to light a low-power bulb.

At the microscopic level, the outstanding feature of the brain is the neurons, at least 15,000 million of them (1.5×10^{10}). Each neuron has its associated axon, some relatively short, others remarkably long (up to several feet); each axon bears numerous branching dendrites, up to 10,000 or more; each dendrite ends in a synapse, through which it communicates with another neuron (Figures 4 and 5).

The total number of intercommunications in the brain is very hard to assess; it has been put at values varying between 10^{13} and 10^{15}. It is difficult to grasp the meaning of such magnitudes. Denton (1985) has attempted to provide an impression of this number by the following analogy: Imagine a vast forest one million square miles in area, planted with trees at a density of 10,000 per square mile; and suppose each tree has 100,000 leaves. Then the number of leaves in the entire forest is 10^{15}, the same number as the interconnections within a human brain. The cell bodies of the neurons make up the "grey matter" of the brain; the axons and dendrites are the "white matter." For more recent research on neuronal networks, see the review by Georgiana Ferry (1987).

The nerves are wrapped in a fatty myelin membrane for insulation, but nerves are *not* the biological equiva-

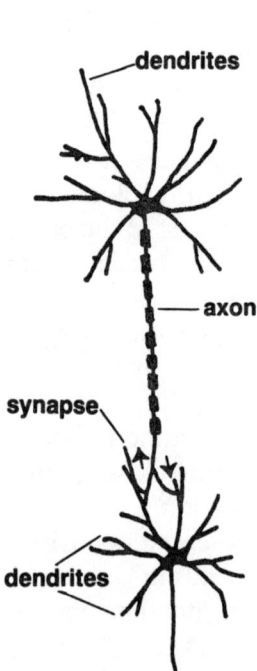

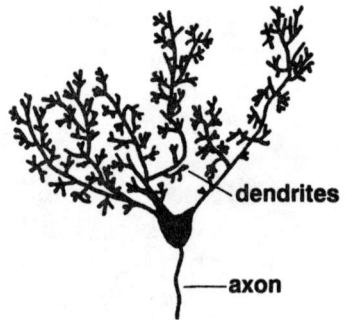

Fig. 4 (left). A nerve cell or neuron. The long nerve fiber or axon branches at the end into multiple dendrites. At the other end, there is a gap or synapse between the axon and dendrites from a nearby neuron.

Fig. 5 (above). A neuron from the cerebellum. Note the many dendrites and the elaborate branching.

lent of wires carrying electrical current, as formerly believed. Electrical potentials, voltages, are indeed involved, but nerve impulses traveling along the axons at about 100 meters per second (250 miles per hour) involve a complex biological phenomenon. The nerve fiber or axon is not freely permeable to sodium and potassium ions. In the resting state, the potassium concentration within the nerve is higher than it is in the surrounding fluid, and the sodium concentration is correspondingly lower within the axon. This ionic imbalance creates an electrical potential across the dividing membrane, amounting to -70 microvolts. A long axon carries about a million "ion-pumps," which can actively transfer potassium and sodium ions either way across the membrane. So when a neuron "fires," the first pump expels some potassium and admits some sodium, lessening the potential to − 40 microvolts. The second pump follows suit, and so on right down the whole axon. Behind this fast wave of ionic transfers, the ion pumps in turn reverse the transfers back to the normal condition. It is this incredibly rapid wave of sodium-potassium transfers forth and back that *constitutes* the nerve impulse when a neuron fires.

When it reaches a synapse, the impulse is passed on to an adjacent synapse on another dendrite, by a quite different mechanism. The transmitting synapse releases a tiny amount of a chemical substance called a neurotransmitter. This is picked up by a protein receptor molecule on the receiving synapse, and the second nerve is triggered. A message from the brain to a muscle, for example, may pass via several of these synaptic junctions. The sequence of operations may seem incredibly complex, but the versatility of the system is actually greater than this preliminary description suggests. The number of neurotransmitting chemicals is more than just one or a few; at least thirty are already known, and more are likely to be discovered. Chemically they are hormones, amino acids, or small peptides (compounds containing a small chain of chemically linked amino acids). Probably only one is released at a specific synapse, but jointly they appear to transmit subtly different messages. Moreover the recipient nerve fiber may be inhibited, i.e., its activity is damped down instead of being stimulated. Further details are deferred to later chapters.

The nervous system is classified in various overlapping ways. There is a set of cranial nerves connected to the sense organs; they include not only sensory but motor nerves, controlling eye movements for example. Spinal nerves control body movements; they are bunched together at particular sites as plexuses. The central nervous system and peripheral nervous system are obviously defined by location. The autonomic nervous system is defined and subdivided by function. It controls all those movements that proceed without conscious thought. Obvious examples are breathing, the beating of the heart, and the functioning of many other organs. But the autonomic system also looks after all habitual and learned body movements like walking, cycling, finding the keys in touch typing, piano playing, even performing standard strokes in games like tennis.

The autonomic system has two chief divisions. The sympathetic system (controlled mainly by the hypothalamus and its medulla) has protagonist or arousing functions. The parasympathetic system (controlled mainly by the midbrain pons and medulla) has antagonistic or calming functions. For example, the sympathetic can accelerate the heartbeat, while the parasympathetic slows it down. It is generally supposed that such activities are immune from conscious cerebral control. But as we shall see later, techniques are available through which conscious control of autonomic functions can be regained. This can be useful in treatment of illness and modification of moods (see Chapter 15).

Each day vast numbers of our neurons wear out and cease to operate. The human brain appears to have no capability for replacing such defunct neurons. It has been said dramatically that our brains begin to die very slowly from the moment we are born. Recent research shows that neuron regeneration did occur in some birds; but in later work it was found that this was not the case in primates nor presumably in man. However, it seems that the brain, like other organs and muscles, can be maintained in fit condition by use and exercise. The person who retires without serious interests beyond work and entertainment is apt to slump gratefully into his armchair in front of the television and to bask in idleness;

he then rapidly deteriorates in both body and mind and is likely to die within a few years. Slow falling off in energy and mental agility is inevitable with advancing years, but the aging process can be held at bay in large degree by cultivating appropriate hobbies and suitable exercise, and above all by cultivating the mind with serious reading and active thinking.

Résumé

Basic information is provided concerning the numerous distinct compartments of the human brain and their functions. The 1.5×10^{10} neurons communicate with one another and with the sense organs, muscles, and all parts of the body by nerve impulses. Within nerves these are waves of changes in electrical potential involving transfers of sodium and potassium ions. Between the synaptic nerve terminals, messages pass by discharge and reception of chemical neurotransmitters. There may be as many as 10^{15} such nerve junctions. Brain activity consumes about 20% of the total energy derived from food. The subdivisions of the two main nervous systems are described.

3

Brains and Computers

The computer is totally unable to make aesthetic, artistic or moral judgments. The spiritual life can never be mechanized.

E. Lester Smith

Can computers think? Answers to this popular question range from emphatic "yes" to emphatic "no." Enthusiastic artificial intelligence researchers say that of course computers can think; wait till we have perfected the fifth generation and sixth generation machines, and they will be thinking better than we can. Not so, skeptics fiercely aver; of course computers cannot think. They are just machines with only a single basic faculty, namely switches that are either on or off. They have no understanding, no intelligence, though they can be programmed to mimic intelligence. John Searle, the 1984 Reith Lecturer on BBC radio, put it in more precise language: "Computers know only syntax...brains understand semantics and meaning." But as John Maddox commented editorially in *Nature*, "that is all right as far as it goes, but it does not go very far." He also pointed out that the controversy is not just academic but has practical importance; an earlier failure to get the right answer may have set Great Britain back some ten years in progress towards better computers.

The wise response to an ill-framed question is a counter-question: "What exactly do you mean? Let us have some definitions." To the question "Can computers think?" the appropriate response would be, "What do you mean by thinking?" After all, entire books have been written about thinking, so the word must have many shades of meaning. The contradictory answers may, after all, both be right if they are based on opposite extremes of this range of connotations. At one end of this range are the views taken, for example, by an ardent practitioner of yoga, or a university graduate whose greatest joy is to write complex computer programs. They might claim that nothing less than original creative thought deserves to be called thinking. At the other extreme, the "man in the street" assumes that thinking covers anything that comes into his head. He may merely repeat, parrot-like, what he read in the newspaper or what the shop steward of his union said; but he might well be prepared to fight anyone who said differently, and he might go on strike and lose wages for the sake of some sacred principle he had enunciated. He would be deeply insulted if anyone told him he was not thinking. Since this sort of thinking is far more common than the creative kind, it must be valid to accept it as an example of genuine thinking.

Now it is easy to answer the original question. Obviously computers are quite incapable of original creative thought. The crucial issue is that they cannot *understand* the meaning of their output. This is true of present electronic machines, and will still be true of any more competent machines based on the same principles. Maddox argues that if we could design a computer just like a brain, then of course it would be able to understand its thoughts. But such an achievement is in practice un-imaginable given the enormous complexity of brains; moreover, Maddox ignores the mind behind the brain and the self behind the mind. Even if we could make an accurate synthetic replica of a brain, I believe it would not be of much use unless it could be "ensouled" by a highly intelligent living entity. So I maintain my belief that no future man-made computer will ever be able to produce and comprehend original creative thoughts.

However, if we accept instead the commonplace con-cept of thinking, then certainly computers already available can do far better than this. So by the pragmatic test of performance, and without resorting to any prin-ciple or preconceived ideas, we must concede that modern computers *can* think, or at least they can *mimic* human thinking rather convincingly. On this kind of pragmatic basis, we can agree that something approach-ing artificial intelligence is indeed in prospect, though it must work on an "as if" level. The machines will never understand what they have been taught to do; never-theless they can be of enormous practical value. Quali-tatively, computers can never approach the capabilities of a trained human mind, but quantitatively they already far surpass the human brain in their fantastic speed of operation.

HUMAN VERSUS MACHINE THINKING

Human and machine thinking proceed along quite different lines. Commonplace human thinking is inex-tricably linked with emotion; indeed it is often initiated and driven by the emotional nature (see Chapter 10). Truly original, creative thinking tends to be initiated and driven by a superior human faculty, the intuition. But again, emotion is also involved. Even in the field of pure abstract mathematics, the researcher tackles a problem because of an emotional urge to do so, and he registers intense pleasure when he succeeds in solving the abstruse problem he has set himself. Human thinking rarely proceeds on strictly logical lines, although some scientists like to believe that it does. The mind is often illogical and irrational; it may proceed in a disjointed manner, turning aside to consider some remembered idea that has come up and which may have a bearing on the original line of thinking. Edward de Bono, head of the International Center for Creative Thinking in New York, has shown that such "lateral thinking" is worth encouraging in problem-solving (de Bono 1985).

By contrast, from its nature a computer is totally amoral, soulless, and unemotional. If it can be said to think, then it exhibits pure rational thought. However, it can mimic creativity if it has been programmed to display "contingency thinking." That is to say, it can be taught, for example, that if the result of a computation is A, it should follow sequence P; if B, then sequence Q; if C, then R, and so forth. If I wished to anthropomorphize a computer, I would choose as a simple example the electronic typewriter that I am using. I would accuse it of dumb insolence! It is like having an employee who adheres exactly to regulations, sullenly and inflexibly. It does *precisely* what I tell it to do, whether it is what I really want or not. If I happen to touch a wrong key, it instantly does what I have directed it to do, and I must find a way to correct the error. Another time it will stubbornly refuse to do what it is capable of doing because I have omitted to press the code key for that operation. On the other hand, it is totally reliable, provided I remember every word of the instruction manual.

The contrast between human thinking and machine thinking is best appreciated by playing board games with a computer as opponent. With the simplest games like tic-tac-toe, the program is straightforward and the computer *never* loses. The human player will lose if his concentration lapses for a single move; the best he can ever achieve is a draw. With games of intermediate complexity a well-programmed computer can beat a human player of world championship class. Only with a game as complex as chess does the human player stand a chance. The early chess programs could be beaten fairly easily, but increasing sophistication in the programming, and more importantly, increases in computing speed have changed the situation. The human player considers several possible next moves that his opponent might make. For each of these he devises appropriate responses, and so on for the next three or four moves. A modern computer works so fast that it may be able to look ahead for as many as twenty moves, swiftly eliminating every unprofitable move to save wasting time on it. The result is impressive, but stolid and wooden in approach. The human player has the advantage of an intuitive feel for the progress of the game, but he has the disadvantages not only of very much slower pace, but of lapses of concentration and occasional failure to appreciate his opponent's line of play. The upshot is that the best computer programs will usually beat all players below Grand Master level.

A detailed and revealing analysis of this situation by Fred Hapgood was published in *New Scientist* under the bold title "Computer Chess Bad—Human Chess Worse" (Hapgood 1982). As Hapgood reports, "The machines do not play good chess; in fact they play *terrible* chess. In any single game, a computer will make enough mistakes to illustrate a whole textbook of what *not* to do. Their play is clumsy, inefficient, diffuse, and just plain ugly. But this does not mean they do not win; as I can testify, they do. But they win not because they can play chess, which they cannot, but because they can beat humans." It appears that even excellent human players make far more serious mistakes than they believe they do; several times in a game they may exhibit astonishing blind spots. The machine's strategy is weak, but it is consistent, so it can take ruthless advantage of all such human errors, and eventually it usually wins the game, "despite an intrinsic quality of play that is so inane as to be comic, as is readily apparent when two computers play each other. They see things that I miss and miss things that I see. It is like playing chess with a Martian; eerie and weird and very interesting." This inevitably means, however, that the computer's game is dull and protracted; presumably it also means that playing against a computer will do little to improve one's standard of play against human competitors.

The *New Scientist* article goes on to describe the programming methods in some detail. It is necessary to allocate scores to possible moves, to enable the computer to choose the highest before proceeding to the next step, and to enable it to reject low-scoring lines of play. To a limited extent, the computer can be taught to improve its play by experience; but its routines for evaluating moves remain basically crude and do not approach the subtlety of the human player. What the best machines can do is to calculate scores for about 100,000 positions per second, which is incomparably faster than the human brain can function. Despite all efforts, it has not proved possible to devise machines that can operate at the levels of ideas, generalizations, and expectations. Human players do operate like this, but the technique evidently leads to far more imprecision than had been supposed; the dim-witted machines exploit this situation with their swift, precise calculations.

A vast amount of time has been expended on the devising and improving of chess-playing software. Apart from financial returns from sales of computers and programs, this effort has been justified in two ways. First the exercise might throw new light on the ways that human brains work. This expectation has not been realized; rather the result has been that we now know more clearly how very different computers are from human brains and minds. Secondly, devising these sophisticated programs might provide useful experience in writing complex programs for more important practical purposes. Doubtless this has happened. One objective was to devise computers that function more like human brains. This is a long way from achievement, though some small advances have been made. For example, some long, repetitive calculations can be broken down in such a way that several subroutines are computed *simultaneously* and the results combined later; this reduces overall computing time without faster chips. But of course parallel processing of many inputs simultaneously is precisely what human brains do constantly as a matter of course and seemingly without effort. An example may be given in relation to information processing, the subject of the next chapter. In one's appreciation of a pastoral scene, various senses come into play. The eyes note the hills and valleys, the trees and grass. The nose enjoys the scent of a flowering shrub. The ears can hear bird song and the rustle of leaves in the breeze. One may reach out a hand to feel the texture of the bark of a tree. All these sense impressions are conveyed to the brain for parallel recording, assessment, and coordination before being passed on to the mind for appreciation as a composite picture.

The greatest expectations for artificial intelligence were that robots driven by computers could be devised, capable of constructing other computers. The nearest approach to this objective seems to be the humdrum use of robots to do soldering or welding jobs on assembly lines.

We may reflect that human bodies and brains already have self-replicating capabilities, through the commonplace operation of sexual reproduction. The fact that all the endeavors of human intelligence have failed to achieve self-replicating machines should have led, one might suppose, to the hypothesis of some superhuman Cosmic Intelligence operating in the biological field to produce vastly more intricate self-replicating organisms. It is not suggested that this Intelligence attends to the construction of every individual component of each body, but that it laid down the basic rules and the mechanisms for development and evolution that science is slowly and painstakingly revealing (see for example Denton 1985). Increasing numbers of scientists, especially physicists, are indeed propounding such hypotheses.

Another example of the fallibility of computers concerns their use in "futurology" programs. It would be helpful if we could look ahead accurately to determine what human civilization will be like in future centuries if present trends continue, or if they change in specified ways. A computer can indeed give us answers—of a sort. The famous "Club of Rome" published the results of such an attempt at computer forecasting. This report received much publicity, and the media approach in most instances was that if a computer reached such conclusions, then they must be right. But later, other research groups fed into computers different initial assumptions about trends and their interaction. Naturally these computer forecasts were quite different from the earlier ones. As the history of forecasting shows, we *cannot* fortell the future; trends alter in ways that we fail to predict, and it is naive to hope that computers might succeed where we have failed. Nevertheless, computers can be useful if we remain aware of their limitations. They *can* work out swiftly what *would* happen *if* a particular group of trends interacting in plausible ways *did* continue unchanged. Since the usual forecast is some sort of disaster, we should wisely conclude that some trends must be altered, if civilization is not to collapse eventually. But this was already obvious before the exercise started!

To sum up, computers deploy brute force and speed; brains deploy subtlety. It is not fruitful nor indeed meaningful to assess which approach is "best." Their skills are different and complementary; *together* they make a good team. Computers can supplement brains and minds, but should never be expected to displace them, even in the distant future. We have nothing to fear from computers unless we deliberately misuse them. We must never delegate decisions to computers, for there are few human problems that can be resolved satisfactorily by heartless calculators, totally devoid of moral principles, sympathy, and human understanding.

My strictures about the intellectual capabilities and heartlessness of computers are reinforced by a recent book from H. L. and S. E. Dreyfus (1986). They propose a model comprising five stages of skill acquisition. Computers can mimic these up to the third stage (competence); but the fourth and fifth, intuition and know-how, are beyond computerization. "Intelligent human behavior is not amenable to formalization in the way required by digital computers."

Resumé

The quality of human thinking varies enormously. Measured against the commonplace level of emotion-driven small talk and repetitions of secondhand opinions, computers undoubtedly *do* think, and better than at this level. But the highest levels of creative thinking, enlightened by intuition, far surpass anything the most sophisticated computer can ever achieve. Chess-playing computers well illustrate the situation. They can usually beat any player below Grand Master standard, but only because of his occasional lapses, which are ruthlessly exploited by the stolid, totally uninspired, but very fast computer. Computers cannot foretell the future; they can only provide projections of trends and interactions guessed at by their users. They are invaluable adjuncts to human thinking but cannot replace it. They are incapable of originality, or of aesthetic or value judgments.

4

Information Processing

Each of us lives within the universe—the prison—of his own brain. Projecting from it are millions of fragile sensory nerve fibres, in groups uniquely adapted to sample the complex states of the world about us, heat, light, force and chemical composition. That is all we ever know directly; all else is logical inference.

Sensory stimuli reaching us are transduced at peripheral nerve endings, and neural replicas of them dispatched brainwards, to the great grey mantle of the cerebral cortex. We use them to form dynamic and continually updated neural maps of the external world, and of our place and orientation, and of events, within it. At the level of sensation, your images and my images are virtually the same, and readily identified one to another by verbal description, or common reaction.

Beyond that, each image is conjoined with genetic and stored experiential information that makes each of us uniquely private. From that complex integral each of us constructs at a higher level of perceptual experience his own, very personal, view from within.

Mountcastle

The brain is so closely coordinated with sense perceptions on the one hand and with muscular activity on the other that we are normally unaware of the details of how this works. We operate like superbly well-integrated robots, but with self-conscious comprehension in addition. So it is instructive to analyze the multitude of steps involved.

By way of illustration, we may consider all that is comprised in an everyday event such as a shopping trip. We stop in front of a shop and see something at the back of the display window that we might want to buy, perhaps a television receiver. This "seeing" that we take for granted (unless we have poor eyesight) is really an exceedingly complex process. The object, illuminated by sunlight or artificial light, reflects colored rays of light into the pupils of the two eyes. Passing through the eyeballs, the rays are refracted and focused by the lenses to make inverted images on the retina at the back of each eye. The cones of the retina each contain one of three pigments corresponding to the three primary colors. These are chemically changed by the light, and this causes signals to pass up the thick bundle of nerves, the optic nerve, that connects the eyes to the brain. Peripheral vision is dealt with by a slightly different mechanism via the rods at the outer edges of the retinas.

Before the nerve impulses reach the brain, they are sorted out to some extent by the eyes, functioning as little extensions of the brain. Because there are some 200 times as many light-sensitive cones in the retina as there are individual optic nerves, some discrimination has to be made by the eyes, such that only the more significant parts of the image pass on to the brain. But even so, this transfer is by no means a straightforward operation. The image from each eye is split vertically; then the images from *both left-hand* halves of the retinas are combined and sent to the *right* half of the brain; similarly the images from *both right-hand* halves of the retinas cross over to the *left* half of the brain. On the way they pass through several ganglia or relay stations, where some further sorting-out and sharpening occurs before the images are eventually displayed by the firing of neurons on the cortex of the brain. They appear in the visual areas of the cortex in both right and left hemispheres of the brain. But the arrangement of these cortical "images" is quite unlike that of the "photographic" images on the retinas. Each half of the brain contains only half the image, that from the opposite sides of the retinas; moreover the image is grossly distorted and rearranged, with the areas near the center of the visual field enlarged in relation to the peripheral parts. Now, we must presume, the mind scans this pair of half-images, rearranging them into the three-dimensional picture we perceive in the "mind's eye." All this happens in the course of a very small fraction of a second, so that we can become aware of a changing panorama of scenes. The impression of depth arises stereoscopically because the two eyes receive slightly different images due to their spatial separation. The same effect permits judgment of distance, though other clues are also used. The object in the shop window is perceived to be near the back mainly from the arrangement of the display, nearer objects partially obscuring those behind. Moreover, from long practice the mind presents us with a three-dimensional picture even when one eye is covered; depth judgment is, however, somewhat impaired in monocular vision.

This account, complex though it may be, is still grossly oversimplified in many respects. An important feature is that the vision presented to the mind's eye is partially "predigested," so to speak. We have noted how the eye and the ganglia edit the visual image on its way to the visual cortex. Also displayed on appropriate areas of the cortex, and doubtless also edited en route, are the relevant corresponding messages from other senses, particularly those of hearing and touch. In addition, the brain has a "standing order" from the mind to search its memory bank and to present relevant memories of similar events. The brain can do all this in a split second, but it can do no more. Like our familiar electronic com-

puter, it is a mindless biocomputer, miraculous though
its capabilities are. Thus, it is the mind that scans all
this information, coordinates and interprets it, makes
sense of it, and in turn presents its understanding to the
conscious self. Finally, it is this personal self that decides
what use to make of the total, fully digested information. It may command the mind and brain to commit
it to memory. It may decide that some action is called
for, which it proceeds to initiate. In the example chosen,
it would decide that the object in the shop window was
a television receiver and that it might be worth buying.
We can know that all this is so by analyzing the whole
experience. Moreover, when we do see something totally
new and unexpected, it comes with a sense of shock and
a "look out" message, sometimes with the automatic reaction of fear. The artist is supposed to view the scene
just as it is, with the "innocent eye" free from all pre-
judgments, but this is very difficult to achieve. It is also
important to recognize that what we thus receive directly
is a *subjective* mental impression. We then proceed to
impose it, with all its imperfections and modifications,
upon the world "out there." Then we proclaim that it
provides us with accurate objective visual information
about the external world.

PASSIVE AND ACTIVE SENSE PERCEPTION

The process described above happens in the automatic, *passive* mode of vision. If we are interested in
what we see, then we react positively, we take an active attitude towards it, we do something about it. Then
seeing becomes looking or watching. We may seek out
additional details that the eyes did not take in at first
glance. In order to do this, we may be obliged to initiate muscular action. Specifically, we may command the
eye muscles to adjust the lens and focus more accurately while we take in a more complete picture; for exam-

ple we may read the description of the object or the price tag and note the features of the particular model of TV receiver offered.

Naturally it takes time to build up a new image on the visual cortex strong enough to draw the attention of the conscious mind; it has been shown that the interval is about half a second. We can perhaps dismiss a suggestion that the mind somehow antedates this small delay by some sort of precognition. When we open closed eyes to view a scene, we are actively conscious of momentary delay before we make sense of what is before our eyes. Again, if something quite unexpected happens, we even have time to think "whatever is that?" before we can make out what we are seeing.

The situation is different when the mind is already alert and viewing a changing scene, as when we turn the eyes or the head or watch a film or television picture. Then we are almost instantaneously at least aware of the raw uninterrupted vision, either through precognition or because the time delay in such circumstances is well below $\frac{1}{10}$th of a second. Studies of subliminal images show that there must be some delay, but that it is very brief. If an altogether different image is displayed on the screen for only one or a few frames, we are not consciously aware of it, though the new image may still register at some unconscious level (whence it may be recoverable by hypnotic regression). Normally the pictures on successive frames differ only slightly, so the conscious mind is well able to follow the events portrayed by concentrating on these small changes. (Incidentally, when we speak of persistence of vision in relation to film or television, we may assume that it is the cortical image that persists, not the retinal one; the eye presumably utilizes the blanks between frames to reconvert the visual pigments back to their receptive chemical states.)

Thus far we have considered only sight. The other senses also operate in complex ways to convey their messages to specific regions of the cortex. These areas have been delineated in patients whose skulls have been opened for necessary surgical treatments. Gentle stimulation of the appropriate area of exposed cortex elicits sensations of sound, taste, or whatever. For hearing the mechanism has been elucidated in considerable detail, but for other senses, that of smell for example, there is still no clear understanding of the way the mechanisms operate.

For all the senses, not only for sight, there are both passive and active modes of functioning. We are usually vaguely and passively aware of the sounds and odors around us. When we eat we are vaguely conscious of the agreeable (or unpleasant) flavor of our food, but how often do we set out to distinguish the ingredients of a dish from its texture and taste, and try to determine what spices and herbs were used to flavor it? Usually we remain passive; we waste the opportunity to take an active interest in our food, to savor it fully, to take advantage of this readily available source of enjoyment. We know about these possibilities, for there are words in our language to distinguish the passive and active modes, though we seldom think about them. They are set out in the table below:

Sense	Passive Mode	Active Mode
Sight	Seeing	Looking, viewing, watching, gazing, observing
Hearing	Hearing	Listening, musical appreciation
Smell	Smelling	Sniffing, appreciation of scents, nosing (of wine)
Taste	Tasting	Tasting (deliberately), gustating, savoring
Touch	Feeling	Palpating, touching, fondling, appreciation of texture

Besides the familiar five senses, there are others, such as proprioception or general awareness of the body and balance.

Another sense is that of direction, well developed in migratory and homing animals and in aborigines and some African tribes, but poorly in civilized people. This turns out to be a highly composite sense. The correct direction may be found in three ways: 1) piloting, the recognition of landmarks; 2) orienting, by sun or stars or the earth's magnetic field; and 3) navigating, taking cognizance of numerous cues, as needed for distant migrations. For fish the "landmarks" may be the smell of waters from different rivers and ocean currents. Some birds and bees orient by the sun, which involves allowing for its apparent traverse across the sky. On overcast days they can sense instead the plane of polarization of sunlight. Nocturnal migrants use the stars; they can even orient correctly indoors in a planetarium. Numerous species appear to have built-in magnetic compasses. Minute rods of magnetite have been found in the brains of fish, birds, and amphibians and in the abdomens of bees. These creatures misorient in a zero magnetic field when surrounded by Helmholtz coils or in a "false" field induced by attached magnets. Some human subjects also showed this effect. People and homing pigeons may also have used dead reckoning or inertial navigation, conscious or unconscious, while they were blindfolded during journeys to the homing point. Some species are sensitive to and may use low-frequency sound waves (infrasound), generated by wind over mountain ranges and ocean wave formations (Dunbar 1984). Redundancy seems to be the keynote in direction-finding; when preferred cues are unavailable or inadequate, others take their place.

Further, some people display various kinds of heightened awareness or extrasensory perception, such as telepathy, nonphysical touch and vision, and intuitive understanding. Sometimes we experience synaesthesia, a synthesis of messages from several senses. For example, if we come upon a wild garlic plant while rambling in the country, we could see it and simultaneously feel the smooth, firm texture of the leaves, pluck and taste its pungency, and smell the fragrance of its flowers, all while we hear the rustle of the wind in the trees; we experience sensual, emotional, and intellectual pleasure, and even perhaps spiritual uplift, all in a single moment. Such are the capabilities of the human brain, mind, and consciousness. There are further modes of communion with our inmost being and with the world, to be discussed in later chapters. They include intuition and ecstasy, culminating in the mystical experience. But to extract the full appreciation of events, we need to be alert and attentive. Often we are inattentive, "lost in thought" as we say, daydreaming. In prayer or meditation we may deliberately withdraw attention from the senses; they continue to function and pass their messages to the brain and may even register in memory, but not in waking consciousness. Only a small fraction of the activity that goes on in the brain is ever reported to consciousness. The brain is forever busy, consuming around 20 watts of energy—but we can still have peace of mind.

Four levels of attention and inattention can be distinguished, well illustrated by listening to music. The first is full attention, conscious appreciation, being "all ears," going out to meet the sound, with the brain in beta rhythm (see Chapter 8) and the "attention center" turned on. In relaxed alpha rhythm, with the attention center off, the music can still be enjoyed, being heard passively as a rather more vague general impression. The third level is that of half-hearing "background music," while the mind is paying more attention to something else. The fourth level is one of total *in*attention to the music, with the mind in beta rhythm again, engrossed in some other activity. One may then be quite startled when the music stops and is replaced by applause. This is the same as the first stage, but something other than the music is the focus of concentrated attention.

SUBJECTIVE AND OBJECTIVE EXPERIENCE

Another confusing aspect of information processing is our attitude towards subjective and objective experience. Many scientists look askance at understanding gained through introspection. This is subjective experience, and they tend to dismiss it as "merely subjective." They place more value upon objective experience, that which comes to us through eyes, ears, and other sense organs. Most highly prized is "factual experience," that which comes from scientific instruments. These valuations seem less secure when we analyze them further. The three types of experience are shown at the top of columns A, B, and C respectively in the table below. Their characteristics as commonly accepted appear in the second horizontal line. In lines 3 and 4 they are analyzed more critically.

Analysis of Types of Experience

A Introspective	B Sensual	C Factual
Subjective Direct Private	Objective Indirect Public	Instrumental Doubly Indirect Public

Subjective experiences arise directly within the consciousness: we have them, we know we have them; they are undeniable. Visual observations (and all other sense impressions) register in the brain and are accessible to the attentive mind. What then appears in consciousness is, in the last analysis, a subjective experience, arising *indirectly* via these fallible steps. The eyes may fail to see all there is to be seen, and the mind may ignore or misinterpret part of what is seen. In any event, the eye responds to only a severely limited segment of the electromagnetic spectrum. Scientific instruments can respond to wider ranges of the spectrum and with greater precision. But the instrumental readings have to be read by the eye; even if they are printed out, the message has to be read. So again what is finally available is a subjective experience involving even more steps of questionable reliability.

Even that is not the end of the matter, as the fourth horizontal line suggests. Subjective experiences are private; except possibly by telepathy, empathy, and so forth, nobody else can know what is in my consciousness. Moreover, although subjective experiences are *real*, they may not be *relevant*. We can create them by imagination; they arise in dreams, though we seldom accept these as providing reliable information. It takes experience to make the necessary discriminations. Also, supporting evidence must be taken into account. Visual observations, whether direct or via instruments, can sometimes be supported by other senses, usually touch. We do not altogether trust ourselves, however; we like to be reassured by other people who say they have the same experiences. This is possible only with objective observations which are in the public domain, not purely private.

There is nothing new in this analysis. Its present purpose is to emphasize the fact that *everything* we know for ourselves, or learn from others, comes to us either directly or indirectly as a subjective experience. Therefore, we may not rule out direct subjective experience or introspection as valid routes to understanding.

Before experiences can be of scientific value, and before they can be communicated to others, they have to be formulated and compared with previous experiences. If abstract, they must at least be given expression as concrete ideas in the mind for personal use. Usually they must be expressed in words before they can be stored in the memory or be made known to others. At all steps in all routes, errors can enter. We can fool ourselves with our imaginings. Observations can be incomplete or faulty due to the limitations of senses or instruments. Our interpretations can be erroneous due to our inexperience or incompetence. Vigilance and discrimination are imperative, in domestic life just as in scientific investigations. In the light of all these uncertainties, the word "fact" has a hollow ring; anything put forward as "positive fact" should be looked at askance. We may smile at the arrogant self-assurance of nineteenth-century scientists, yet we tend to imitate their stance, to be just as certain that modern science is "right." We should be more humble and open-minded, for this in its turn may be overturned by deeper understanding in the future.

Summarizing this chapter on information processing, I suggest that we can fruitfully divide our complex system of being into four compartments for better understanding. Starting from the outside, as it were, they are: 1) the physical body with its sense organs; 2) the brain, our biocomputer, which processes the sense impressions (it is actually another part of the physical body); 3) the nonmaterial mind which coordinates and understands what the brain presents to it; 4) the nonmaterial conscious self, the seat of will and intention. The next chapter on action coordination provides further evidence for the validity of this subdivision.

Resumé

Our appreciation of the environment via the sense organs is a vastly more complex procedure than we normally suppose. What we are pleased to regard as objective observations are really indirect and subjective; only what we tend to dismiss as subjective impressions are direct. Passive and active sense perceptions can be discriminated. We may need to reconsider what can be regarded as positive fact.

5

Coordinating Action

Mind knows itself and knows the world; chemistry and physics, explaining so much, cannot undertake to explain mind itself.

Charles Sherrington

Some materialists are prepared to use the word "mind" to denote a system that *receives* information from the world via the sense organs and the brain. But the idea of any *reverse traffic*, of instructions given to the brain, is anathema to them. Yet common experience unites with experimental evidence to proclaim that as self-conscious individuals we do give instructions to the brain. This is an extremely important issue which must be considered in some detail. For example, we may think it would be a good idea to go out for a walk, to get some fresh air into our lungs and take some exercise. How does this notion arise within the human psyche? How is it converted into a firm decision? How is the decision translated into action? The body may feel lazy; it may have to be coaxed or bullied a little before it agrees; certainly it does not make the decision. I see the brain as a biocomputer, incapable of initiating decision-making, though it can be preprogrammed to select between alternatives. The mind does participate, but surely the actual decision is made at the fourth level in the hierarchy, the individual himself, the "I" or "self."

Once one has considered the idea of going for a walk and confirmed the decision, then the chain of steps involved in the performance of coordinated muscular activity is the reverse of that involved in sense perception. The conscious self asserts its superior position in the hierarchy of the personality. It decides upon, wills, and initiates an action sequence, passes on its command to the mind, which in turn relays it to the brain and thence to the muscles.

Expressed in the simplest terms, the brain finally issues each command via an impulse in a specialized nerve cell called a motoneurone. Its long axon runs down the spine, then branches out to terminate in motor endplates within its particular bundle of around one hundred muscle fibers. Finally the nerve impulse induces contraction of these muscle fibers. All coordinated muscular actions in the body are organized via a total of some 200,000 such nerve-muscle units. Used in innumerable combinations, they account for all the complex movements that can be made by the body, the limbs, and the digits. The human consciousness need not concern itself with the details, unless it is learning a new manual skill like typing. Even then, it has only to will the use of a particular finger to press a selected key with the proper pressure and timing of impact. The brain automatically selects the appropriate groups of muscle fibers and sends the sequence of nerve impulses that ensures that the action is carried out as intended.

Once learned, these action sequences or motor programs are stored in the brain for subsequent use. In the example of typing, just thinking of the next letter evokes the necessary muscular performance.

NEURAL CORRELATES OF WILLED ACTION

Eccles presents several lines of research that he believes offer conclusive experimental evidence for the sequence of events described above (Popper and Eccles 1977; Eccles 1980). The first of these is a series of experiments by Kornhuber on human subjects in 1974. Under rigorous experimental conditions, subjects willed themselves to perform a specified action when told to do so. A wide-ranging negative potential (the readiness potential) first built up gradually over the top of the brain during about 0.8 seconds; then the potential concentrated on the pyramidal cells that send neural impulses to the motor muscles. Only after all these brain events had been recorded did the required muscular action occur. There is no doubt that in these experiments electrical potentials in the brain were taking place nearly a second before muscular action commenced. However, a possible weakness of these experiments is that some muscular actions result from learned behavior patterns, and no longer require active thought for their initiation. So it is hard to separate these old patterns from newly planned activity that does require conscious thought. Eccles is convinced that such distinctions were made successfully in Kornhuber's research and that the subjects made the desired movements without disturbing environmental influences. Also any random brain potentials were effectively eliminated by averaging hundreds of traces of the brain potentials.

Eccles reported more recent work in this field to a Wrekin Trust conference in Winchester, England, in March 1982. This research has since been reported in a book by Eccles and Daniel L. Robinson, professor of psychology at Georgetown University (Eccles and Robinson 1984). At the conference Eccles spoke of new work on a small area of the cortex now known as the "sup-

plementary motor area" (SMA). This area had been discovered by Penfield some thirty years previously, but
had become a sort of Cinderella area of unknown function. Its stimulation in exposed brains resulted merely
in meaningless writhing movements. The SMA has now
become established as the region of the cortex that coordinates consciously willed muscular movements. It has
the address, so to speak, of all motor programs stored
in the brain, from which it can compile the appropriate
sequence of messages to the muscles needed to complete
the proposed task. Hundreds of millions of neurons are
involved in this complex operation, but it seems that no
simpler mechanism could be devised to enable the body
to carry out, seemingly without effort, the complicated
and varied movements we demand of it.

Even in animals the same system is present, though
possibly in somewhat simplified form, as the following
report of research by Porter of Canberra, Australia, ex-
emplifies. It was done on monkeys that had electrodes
implanted in their SMA and in the motor cortex areas.
The animals were trained to pull a lever, using right or
left paw as they chose; each pull was rewarded by a food
pellet. The recording of brain potentials normally
showed irregular background pulses, but at intervals
these were replaced by regular fast pulses from the SMA
area, followed by firing of motor cortex cells. Then one
half to one second after these recordings started, the
monkey pulled the lever. These experiments provide
clear evidence of mental intention preceding muscular
action.

This was the first of three lines of research reported
by Eccles at the Wrekin Trust conference. The second
concerns experiments on human volunteers, done by
Niels Larsen in Copenhagen in 1980, that clearly showed
results of purely mental activity on the SMA. The subjects were patients attending for an angiogram test,

which involves inserting a needle into the carotid artery
that carries blood to the head. When this test was com-
pleted, and with the patient's consent, the needle was
used to inject radioactive xenon for the experiment. The
whole blood stream was thus made radioactive for the
brief period of the useful life of this radioisotope, namely
about one minute. The subject was fitted with a helmet
carrying an array of 254 counters to measure radioac-
tivity. When any part of the brain is engaged in mental
activity, the blood flow to that region instantly increases
dramatically. Such active areas were detected by the
counters and the results displayed by corresponding
color-coded pixels on a television monitor.

The muscular actions required from the subject were
an intricate ritual of finger and thumb movements deliberately designed to demand intense concentration.
When these were performed, increased mental activity
was recorded on the screen in regions corresponding to
both SMA and motor cortex areas. In such preliminary
stages of the experiment, it was impossible to discern
which area became active first. The brilliantly devised
second stage consisted in asking the subject to *imagine*
that he was doing the finger exercises, but without actually doing them. In other words, activity was solely
at the mental level. When this took place, increased
blood flow was registered *only* in the SMA area, not in
the motor cortex, as Eccles pointed out. This constitutes
a quite conclusive and highly significant demonstration
of purely mental activity willed by the subject in his nonmaterial mind.

The third example given by Eccles is of more recent
work by Kornhuber, on the "readiness potential," the
negative potential that grows for about a second before
actual muscle movement occurs. The new feature in this
was performing the experiment on a patient with Parkinson's disease, in whom muscular coordination is extreme-

ly difficult. If such a subject wished to move a muscle, the readiness potential could be seen building up to the normal strength in the SMA, but there was little or no firing in the motor cortex area, and the intended action could not be made. It is known from other work that messages do not pass directly from the SMA to the motor cortex; impulses travel via the cerebellum and the basal ganglia before reaching the motor area. In Parkinson's disease the route from these basal ganglia to the motor cortex is blocked, so that no effective message can be passed on to the muscles.

The researchers who discovered the prior electrical activity in the SMA were at first puzzled about its significance. They were inclined to look for some still earlier brain activity as the initiating event. If they had found one, what then would have caused it in turn? It was Eccles who pointed out that the prime initiator was nowhere in the brain, but in the immaterial mind.

Even for those who were never in any doubt, it is satisfying to have these stringent scientific proofs that the conscious self, acting through the mind, can and does bring about electrical and chemical activity in the brain, leading to bodily movements. It ought to be enough to convince any materialist, but apparently it is not. The 1984 Reith Lecturer on British radio, John Searle, was still arguing that the brain alone is responsible for everything we think and do.

The work establishing a delay of one half to one second between the conscious self willing an act and its actual performance does leave an important practical problem. Such delay is sometimes intolerable; in this hurried age, mind and brain just have to do better than this! So they do, of course. Even half a second can spell the difference between life and death when driving a car in fast traffic. When reaction times between perception of a crisis and muscular action to avoid it are measured, the delay is found to be only $\frac{1}{10}$ to $\frac{1}{5}$ of a second. So how is this discrepancy to be explained?

Eccles cites experiments by Libet that show conclusively that the delay is real—and puzzling. The rather preposterous suggestion that the gap might be bridged by the ESP faculty of precognition need hardly be seriously entertained. As Eccles himself suggested in his Eddington Lecture of 1965, we may suppose that the swift reaction to an emergency is made automatically by the brain alone. That is to say, it has been preprogrammed to do the right thing in a crisis by calling up the appropriate motor programs. In other words, we respond to an urgent situation before we are even consciously aware of it! This is borne out by common experience in fast games like tennis. It is clearly the body and brain, highly trained by long experience, that play most of the game without deliberation. If the player consciously steps in to countermand the response thus chosen, he usually makes a mess of the shot. Strategy is of course thought out and imprinted on the brain between games, but the actual strokes are best left to "play themselves." Again, in acts of bravery the hero often does the right thing automatically. Praised for his bravery, he may shrug his shoulders and say, "I didn't stop to think; I just went straight in and pulled the man out of the blazing car moments before it exploded." The implication is that if he *had* stopped to think, he would have held back, realizing the extreme danger of death or serious injury to himself. So our unconscious actions may sometimes be nobler than our conscious thoughts.

Once again the story has been oversimplified to facilitate the telling of it. The cerebral cortex does not plan these motor functions in quite the direct manner implied. It calls in, for consultation so to speak, another area of the brain, the cerebellum, which is a powerful subsidiary biocomputer. Impulses travel to this region on a loop circuit, and doubtless return amplified and with program details added.

I submit that the evidence presented in this chapter should suffice to persuade any unbiased person to reject the claims of radical materialists that the brain is solely responsible for all we think and do. The complementary philosophical arguments have been convincingly presented by Robinson in his book written jointly with Eccles (1984).

RÉSUMÉ

Several lines of experimental evidence support the commonsense suppositions about the sequence of events involved in muscular action. The conscious self wills the action, and the command is passed via the mind to the supplementary motor area of the brain. A readiness potential builds up, and about 0.8 seconds later the appropriate nerve impulses induce muscular action. The reaction time in response to a crisis is much shorter, indicating that the brain is making a preprogrammed response on its own initiative.

6

The Mind-Brain Interface

There is no problem about the genetic uniqueness of my brain. It is the uniqueness of the experienced self that requires this hypothesis of an independent origin of the self or soul, which is then associated with a brain, that so becomes my brain.

Sir John Eccles

Earlier chapters have set out a threefold hierarchy of self, mind, and brain to explain our two-way interaction with the environment. This is an awkward sort of hierarchy because its component parts lie partly in the material world and partly in an inner nonmaterial realm. Nevertheless the evidence from common experience, introspection, and experiment seems plausible and convincing; it seems the most satisfactory way to rationalize both the steps involved in sense perception in the intake direction and in voluntary muscular activity in the reverse output direction. To understand these flows in our life-pattern, we seem obliged to postulate these three divisions of our human nature. If we shrink from such analysis and insist upon regarding ourselves only holistically, then we can never satisfy the natural curiosity that most of us experience as to "what makes us tick."

The Liaison Brain

It is necessary to face boldly the strange gap between the material world and the unseen world, between mind and brain, or more broadly between mind and matter. In his books (Eccles and Robinson 1984; Popper and Eccles 1977) Eccles devotes much attention to the problem of how nonmaterial mind can interact with material brain. There needs to be some region of the brain that is exceedingly sensitive and so exquisitely poised that it is able to respond to the minute energy of impulses from the nonmaterial mind; it must be able to amplify these "mind-waves" sufficiently for them to induce firing of material neurons. Eccles claims that just such a region does exist in what he calls "the liaison brain." He uses this term to denote those areas of the cortex, mainly of the dominant hemisphere, that are involved in this interaction. He describes modular structures in the cortex which appear to be uniquely fitted to serve this purpose, to function as a mind-brain interface. Each module is about 3 mm. long and 0.1-0.5 mm. wide, and they are packed together in an arrangement of vertical columns with a total of one to two million modules in the liaison brain. Each module contains around 10,000 neurons, each neuron carrying hundreds, sometimes even thousands of synapses on its axon. Each module is not only anatomically distinct, but also it appears to function as a more or less independent entity, though it has synaptic connections with hundreds of other modules and with other parts of the central nervous system.

The key feature of the entire system seems to be that each module can act as a kind of preamplifier. The tiniest message from the mind, directly affecting perhaps only a handful of neurons in a module, can be built up within its structure, acting as a kind of power unit, until its pyramidal cells can generate impulses strong enough to affect other modules or other regions of the central nervous system.

It is important to note that neurons exhibit both excitatory and inhibitory action. A module that is amplifying and passing on a message from the mind can dominate and suppress modules not so engaged. Each module contains the usual six layers of cells, but the outermost two layers display a finer and more delicate array of neurons than those in the deeper layers. The inhibitory neurons are smaller, exercising less powerful and more diffuse synaptic action upon pyramidal cells, which are the principal components of the modules.

Thus the operations within even a single module are inconceivably complex, far more so than those of the most advanced microchip of electronic computers—and there are a million or two of such modules functioning as an integrated system. Moreover, the functioning of these cortical modules is much more subtle than the simple on-off action of a solid-state transistor. Impulses are graded not only in nature (excitatory or inhibitory) but also in intensity, and a single module can send out hundreds of signals simultaneously, in parallel.

Popper and Eccles conclude that because of the amplifying power of the cortical modules, the initial impulse can be so minute that it need not contravene the First or Second Laws of Thermodynamics. The First Law proclaims the principle of the conservation of energy. The Second Law can be stated in various forms, e.g. "It is impossible for a self-acting machine unaided by any external agency to convey energy from one body to another at a higher temperature." However, in the present situation it appears that any such argument is sterile. By definition the Laws of Thermodynamics apply only to *closed systems,* and it has been pointed out repeatedly that living organisms are *open* systems. The physicist

Erwin Schrödinger expressed this fact dramatically by his statement that "organisms feed upon negative entropy"; i.e. they create organization out of chaos. Thus may the Gordian knot be cut; or rather we show that the tying in the first place was based upon a misconception.

If we feel cheated by this conclusion, if we have a nagging suspicion that the mind-brain problem has still not been resolved, then we should be quite right. The problem is not thus easily dismissed. The notion of an open system must somehow be extended to embrace not just the physical world, but also nonmaterial realms. This is something that materialists obviously cannot concede. To be fair, although Eccles did not pose this genuine issue precisely in these terms, he did face up to it. He argues it out on philosophical grounds; but even more convincingly he claims that it is experimentally proven by the work of Kornhuber and others, as already noted in Chapter 5.

There have been attempts to circumvent the issue altogether. The problem is not resolved by mentally shutting both mind and brain inside a "black box" and affirming that its contents are beyond the scope of scientific enquiry. Nor is it effectively resolved by the mystical approach, by declaring that the concepts of both mind and brain are ultimately subsumed within One Reality, so that there really is no problem. While we go on living in a dualistic world, while as scientists we interest ourselves in the manner in which its components interact, it remains our duty to consider this problem. It may be beyond the boundaries that scientists have arbitrarily set; but that means only that these boundaries need to be extended to include what is now regarded as paranormal.

There are indeed a number of scientists who perceive this need. Parapsychology is now regarded as a legitimate field of research in some universities. Dr. L. J. Bendit was possibly the first to receive a higher degree (M.D.) in this field in 1944 for his book *Paranormal Cognition*. Today, this kind of thing is less unusual. A Chair of Parapsychology has been set up in Edinburgh University, in accordance with a bequest by Arthur Koestler and his wife. Units for research into the paranormal are established in other British and American universities.

The case for mind-brain interaction via the "liaison brain" appears to be well established. However, we are still entitled to ask if this is the *only* part of the brain that has direct communion with the conscious self. Eccles himself seemed a little puzzled to discover that the liaison areas appeared to be limited to the dominant (usually left) hemisphere. Surely the self needs some *direct* access to the minor hemisphere, in addition to the route from the dominant hemisphere via the corpus callosum. Important aspects of human life concern the activities for which the right hemisphere is specialized (see Chapter 7). Can it be that all communications have to be channelled through the dominant hemisphere? This seems intrinsically improbable, and experience tells us that "affairs of the heart," for example, seem to bypass the cool, calculating nature of the left hemisphere; yet the brain can hardly be bypassed altogether.

There is another and quite different side to this problem. The neocortex, which includes the liaison brain, was a relatively late evolutionary development. So how was communication made before this liaison brain even existed as a channel? Primitive organisms can doubtless manage with instinct alone. But higher animals must surely be credited with the ability to consider alternative behavioral sequences, to weigh their likely consequences, to make thought-out decisions, and to act upon them. In order to initiate the appropriate actions, the animal self must be able to communicate with its brain to get the requisite muscles acting. It is not suggested of course that the animal understands how this sequence of events operates. It just knows what it wants to do and does it. After all, that is how *we* operate; we do have the ability to understand the mechanism, but ordinarily we never think about it.

The point at issue is that we still need to discover some more primitive part of the brain that is able to commune with the conscious self. An answer may emerge from the work of Richard Silberstein in Australia. Despite the strong evidence that Eccles has produced for areas of the cortex as the link between brain and conscious self, Silberstein prefers to regard the brain stem as the linking area. He points out that nerve fibers connect the brain stem with all areas of the cortex, providing two-way traffic. He further suggests that the brain stem may be the region where information from all sense organs is integrated before it is presented to the mind (Silberstein). These are persuasive ideas. As will be seen shortly, there is no difficulty about accepting *both* brain stem *and* cortical liaison brain as primary linking regions. In addition, we may suggest that the brain stem is the older part of the brain that provided the sole link before the neocortex was developed.

THE NATURE OF THE INTERFACE

In relation to the mind-brain problem, we are constrained as good scientists to seek to understand the mechanism of the interaction between mind and brain. The word "interface" used by Eccles reminds physicists of the perfectly smooth specular surfaces of water covered by oil, a pool of still water, or a soap bubble. The behavior of such immiscible liquid-liquid or liquid-gas phases in mutual contact is coordinated in the Phase

Rule. But in biological organisms the surfaces at which
discrete systems meet are less abrupt; they tend to be
not so much mathematical surfaces as membranes of significant thickness, within which the two systems merge
into one another. It would not be surprising, therefore,
to find that the "interface" between mind and brain is
similarly an intermediate structure, more like a biological membrane than the abrupt transition of physical
systems. The concept of an "etheric" body and brain provides just such a structure.

The literature of the paranormal speaks of subtle
bodies, etheric and astral, in addition to the physical
body. Apparitions are said to be people conscious in a
subtle body, either while living but in separation (see
Chapter 12), or more often after death. Clairvoyants
perceive the subtle bodies as auras surrounding living
persons. Kilner believed that auras could be seen by normal individuals if the eyes were first sensitized by gaz-
ing at the sky through screens of dicyanine dye solutions
and other colored liquids. He gave detailed descriptions
of many auras he had seen himself in this way, but the
screens do not work for everyone. They probably only
enhance an existing tendency towards this form of extrasensory perception. Further powerful evidence for the
reality of subtle bodies is provided by the many people
who have had out-of-body experiences (see Chapter 12).
People who have had a limb amputated usually have
some personal knowledge of their etheric body through
"phantom limb" experiences; they feel vague sensations
of heat, cold, and pain in the missing limb, but difficult
to locate precisely. Physiologists insist that these come
from the severed ends of nerves at the remaining stump.
There may be truth in this, but it is not the whole story.
For example, if scalding water is applied to the place
where the missing limb would be, the subject will jump

with pain. Possibly this residual sensitivity of the etheric body is a relic from times long past before our present elaborate nervous system existed.

In the present context it is this etheric body, and in particular the etheric brain, that is of interest. The etheric matter of which this body is composed is said to be physical matter of a finer grade than gases. It is customary to state that this etheric matter is not recognized by science. While this is literally true, my own belief is that scientists are already familiar with at least some of the etheric sublevels, but that they quite properly use their own terms for these. Back in the nineteenth century Crookes proposed the term "radiant matter" for states more tenuous than gas. I would go further by suggesting that plasma states and all subatomic particles should be relegated to etheric states of matter.

The obvious corollary that etheric bodies are composed of subatomic particles is liable to be dismissed as absurd. But it is no more so than the statement that the physical body is composed of carbon, hydrogen, oxygen, nitrogen, and a few other elements. Naturally they do not occur as such, but combined into the macromolecules familiar in biochemistry. There seems no reason why appropriate subatomic particles should not similarly be combined into "etheric molecules" not yet recognized by science.

Details of the nature and structure of the etheric body are beyond the scope of this book and can be found in the appropriate literature (see for example Powell 1969 and Bailey 1956). Suffice it to say that it is a highly structured body. Some accounts suggest that it replicates many of the structures of the physical body, particularly the nervous system. Others suggest that its internal arrangements are unique, and that its principal function is to imbibe and distribute prana or vitality to the physical body. An elaborate system of channels or nadis has been described, but these seem more likely to correspond with the meridians of acupuncture practitioners than with the physical nerves.

Thus it might be said that the etheric brain, the physical brain's counterpart in etheric matter, itself comprises the "interface"; it is the link we are seeking between the subtle mind and the material brain. In this light, mind-body interaction seems more plausible and more comprehensible. It does not take place across a sharp interface between physical matter and the subtle realms. Instead mind acts first upon "etheric matter," which is already too tenuous to affect most physical instruments, and in fact is often regarded as itself the lowest of the subtle realms. Yet it must be properly classed as part of the physical world, especially so if, as suggested, it is the domain of subatomic particles. It is then not so surprising if this tenuous kind of matter could be affected by the mind and pass on its messages to the brain, itself the most delicately organized matter in the whole of creation, sensitively poised to respond to the slightest impulses.

The process can perhaps be understood in a little more detail, with the help of creative imagination guided by the books cited. The etheric body is said to be coextensive with the physical body but to extend about 5 mm. beyond the skin. So the etheric brain permeates the whole of the physical brain. Thus, if there are regions additional to the liaison brain through which mind and brain interact, or interacted in earlier evolutionary cycles, this raises no difficulties, since they are all in intimate contact with the etheric brain. In earlier eras, less refined modes of communication, slower to respond and less specific, would have sufficed for the needs of more primitive organisms, and may still suffice for some purposes.

Résumé

Having established the need to postulate a triple hierarchy of self, mind, and brain, we must explain the nature of the interaction between the unseen world of the first two components and the material world. The region of the brain cortex involved in the interchange is the "liaison brain." It contains one to two million richly interconnected modules, each functioning as a miniature biocomputer and preamplifier of mind messages. The liaison brain appears to occur only in the left hemisphere, but other areas of mind-brain interaction must be postulated, in both animals and humans. The "interface" is unlikely to resemble the sharp boundary between physical phases; it is probably more akin to the membranes separating biological systems. It is suggested that the "etheric brain" known to some clairvoyants fulfills this function; also that etheric matter is already known to science in the form of plasma states and subatomic particles. The nature of the etheric body is described briefly.

7

The Two Hemispheres

Man was meant to be a creator, not a collection of
thoughts and procedures attached to a balloon called
ego....Our own culture has been nearly ruined by this
forgetting.

Jacob Needleman

The intriguing story of the two hemispheres of the
brain has hit the popular imagination, and has been the
subject of numerous articles in magazines and even
newspapers. The left hemisphere is said to be concerned
with language, logical and analytical thinking, calcula-
tion, and in general with concrete practical matters. In
contrast, the right hemisphere is concerned with abstract
holistic thinking and with music and other aesthetic activities; in general it is synthetic rather than analytical
and has pictorial, space, and pattern sense. For most
people the left hemisphere is the dominant one, and this
goes with right-handedness because the left hemisphere
controls the right side of the body, and vice versa.

DIVISION WITH INTEGRATION

Enthusiastic lateralists give the impression that they
believe the functions of the two hemispheres are strict-

ly specialized in these ways, and that each hardly knows what the other is doing. Nothing could be further from the truth, and it is important to get the situation into perspective. In the normal brain the two hemispheres are extremely well integrated. They are linked by the corpus callosum, a thick bundle of nerves containing some 200 million fibers. It is as if the hemispheres were joined by a very thick telephone cable, through which torrents of information can pass at great speed in both directions.

Most of our knowledge about the two halves of the brain has come from subjects who are far from normal. They may be epileptics, or they may have suffered brain damage through tumor growth or accident. To deal with these conditions, they have undergone surgical intervention such as severing of the corpus callosum or excision of part or all of one hemisphere. Reports on some of these subjects will be given later in this chapter.

It is interesting to speculate on how the division arose. Many important organs of the body are duplicated, namely the lungs, the brain, the kidneys, breasts, eyes, and ears. For animals the brain is literally duplicated; there is no evidence of specialization of hemispheres even in the higher primates. It seems logical to suggest, therefore, that duplication is an example of planned redundancy in nature, just as we put two or even three computers in a spacecraft, as backup in case the one in use malfunctions. Similarly, we can still function, though less efficiently, if we lose the use of one of our replicated parts. It often happens that when we devise something we think really clever, like providing spares of vital computers, we later come to realize that nature had the idea first. For another instance, the wheel has been hailed as a brilliant invention of early man, but we now know of a tiny pond organism that has a freely-rotating propeller-like flagellum for propulsion.

Differentiation of the functions of the hemispheres

must be a relatively recent evolutionary development. There is archeological evidence that right-handedness did not appear until around 5000 B.C. in the Stone Age, and was not fully established until about 2000 B.C. in the Bronze Age. Right-handedness is of course now associated with left-hemisphere dominance. It has been speculated that it was rock-throwing to kill animals for food that led to increased development of the muscles of the right hand and arm, and thus incidentally to the dominance of the left hemisphere. Specialization of the hemispheres may be presumed to have stemmed from the greater demands made of the brain, arising from increasingly complicated life styles, language, education, abstract thinking, and aesthetic appreciation.

By division of labor, greater overall capacity and efficiency can be achieved. The functions of the two hemispheres are complementary; each contributes its quota to our rich overall understanding of the world, ourselves, and other people. Corresponding with late evolutionary development, specialization arises only during late childhood. There is evidence that in an individual's early years each hemisphere can perform all brain functions. Young people remain normal after the excision of one hemisphere, including the dominant one. Even mature individuals can slowly relearn the performance of all brain functions after the loss of one hemisphere. This phenomenon used to be termed "transference," as if the excised and destroyed hemisphere could transfer its capabilities to the other. Obviously the remaining one must have retained them in latent form, and they were reactivated by training and practice. Complete retraining in adult subjects may take up to a year. We may presume, in line with the main thesis of this book, that rehabilitation is not simply automatic, but is largely organized by the conscious self, working through the mind.

HEMISPHERE SPECIALIZATION AND DOMINANCE

Most of our knowledge of hemisphere specialization derives from subjects who had very severe epilepsy. A "brain storm" of uncontrollable brain activity would arise in a faulty region of one hemisphere and then spread over the whole brain, resulting in distressing epileptic fits. Roger Sperry pioneered a drastic operation that gave dramatic relief from this condition, namely complete severance of the corpus callosum. This cut off the main channel of communication between the two half-brains; subsidiary nerve connections remained, but these were unable to take over the total original communication load. Thus each hemisphere went on doing what it was used to doing, but was unable to communicate effectively with its partner. Superficially, the subjects appeared to behave much as they did before the operation; but Sperry devised ingenious tests to reveal uncoordinated activities of the divided hemispheres.

The setup for these tests comprises a table screened from the subject's view, with assorted objects that he can feel with his hands. There is also a white screen in front of the subject, upon which printed words can be projected, so that they will be seen only in either right or left visual fields of the two eyes; the fields are separated by half-dark spectacles blocking the appropriate fields. Then, for example, if the subject is presented with the word "pencil" in the two left visual fields, the image appears exclusively in the cortex of the right hemisphere. The subject does not know consciously that the word has appeared. Nevertheless his right half-brain has recognized the meaning of the word. If the subject is instructed to pick up the object, he can do so with his *left* hand (controlled by the right half-brain), but not with the right hand. Nor can he name the object, because the language centers are in the left half-brain. In fact the subject is amazed at what his left hand is doing, for he has no conscious knowledge of it and disclaims responsibility for its actions! It is as if he harbored an alien intelligence in his brain, of which he has no direct consciousness.

Another test is for the subject to match a geometrical design by building it up from colored blocks. He can do this easily with his left hand, even though he has no conscious understanding of what he is doing. But the right hand fumbles over the task even though the subject is now conscious of what he is trying to do. This is because the left hemisphere—which is now in sole charge—lacks the spatial sense of pattern recognition; he has no access to the abilities of the right hemisphere in this respect. The right hemisphere can understand the names of common objects, but not ideas; it cannot cope with most verbs. Flashing words like "wave" or "nod" only to the left visual field elicits no response. Also, this part of the brain has little calculating ability. Indeed, the split-brain subject is unaware of all sensual inputs and other happenings in the right hemisphere. Such individuals must presumably be effectively blind in the left visual fields of both eyes; to see objects to their immediate left, they would need to turn the eyes or the head leftwards.

Stan Gooch (1980) has argued forcefully that surgery separating the hemispheres, or commisurotomy, is not really helpful since it leaves the subject confused, with divided half-brains working in competition at cross-purposes rather than in harmony. He concludes from the limited information available that subjects are better off when the damaged hemisphere is completely removed, along with the connecting nerve cable. Then the remaining half-brain eventually becomes a whole brain, even though its total capabilities may be somewhat diminished.

It is certain that normal subjects do not behave in any such manner as those who have suffered commisurotomy. Normally, the two hemispheres are very well coordinated. Nevertheless, it is also certain that specialization does occur; confirmation is available from normal adults. For example, if normal subjects are fitted with earphones and *different* words are fed simultaneously to the two ears, it is the word sounding in the right ear that is usually heard and recalled. This is because nearly all the input to the right ear crosses over to the left hemisphere, which attends to language processing. Similarly, if vertical partitions are erected to separate the right and left visual fields of both eyes, then printed words are recognized more quickly if they are presented to the right visual fields, again because the information from both right fields crosses over to the left hemisphere.

Conversely, one might expect the aesthetic enjoyment of music to be enhanced if it were fed into the left ear only, since the sound would be processed in the right hemisphere which is appropriately specialized. In practice, as experience with stereophonic music divided between right and left earphones has taught us, appreciation of music is (or can be) a holistic accomplishment in which the overall direct enjoyment capabilities of the right hemisphere are combined with the more analytical approach of the left hemisphere. Indeed, I have suggested elsewhere that listening to classical music in this way may encourage hemispheric coordination. It is often said that Western culture, oriented towards science, technology, and rational thinking, tends to overdevelop the left hemisphere, increasing its dominance. This should be counterbalanced by artistic and aesthetic pursuits.

A new slant to the notion of dominance is provided by recent work in several American laboratories. Most people breathe through only one nostril, the other being mildly congested; periodically a changeover occurs

automatically (every two hours or so) (Rendell 1974).
It now appears from EEG measurements that conges-
tion signals partial abeyance of the opposite hemisphere;
that is to say, a clear nostril is correlated with temporary
dominance of the contralateral hemisphere. It seems that
it is not necessary to accept this situation passively.
Forceful breathing through the congested nostril can
clear it, and presumably the related hemisphere can be
brought back into temporary dominance. If a session
of active thinking is projected while the right nostril is
blocked, then clearing it should reactivate the appropriate left hemisphere. Conversely, prior to rest and
relaxation the left nostril may usefully be cleared, if
necessary.

These observations may perhaps be related to the
Hatha Yoga practice of the bellows breath, i.e., inhal-
ing through one nostril with the other occluded, and
then exhaling through the other nostril, repeating the
cycle six times or so. My own experience after some seven
years of this practice is that both nostrils remain clear
most of the time. Whether this is a cause-and-effect relationship cannot be determined from this single case.
However it does seem possible that the objective of this
practice is indeed holistic integration of the two halves
of the brain, so that both are always on duty, ready to
cope jointly with any situation. The ideal would seem
to be balanced development of the two hemispheres with
neither in dominance over the other. It might be supposed that this situation, if fully attained, would lead
to ambidexterity. Conversely, deliberate exercises designed to promote ambidexterity should lead to aboli-
tion of hemisphere dominance.

Recent research has thrown some doubt on the notion that the left hemisphere tends to analyze incoming
information, while the right makes holistic appraisals.

New evidence suggests rather that the left hemisphere excels at the detailed processing of information; it reads the small print, so to speak. The right, in contradistinction, is more adept at making a rapid overall assessment of the larger features, even adding a few guesses in the process; but nevertheless it is the more accurate in sizing up images presented for only a brief instant or those of poor quality. The left hemisphere does a more thorough job, provided it is given enough time; it can fill in and rectify the hasty assessment of the right hemisphere. It may turn out that the somewhat contradictory conclusions were each made on too few cases. Some of the subjects were abnormal anyhow (epileptics). It seems entirely feasible that individual variations occur in the precise manner in which our two hemispheres become specialized—just as we differ in temperaments.

It is usually said that the right hemisphere is the seat of our emotional nature. Other studies claim that the left is also involved in emotional responses, especially to positive, happy, optimistic states; the right responds more to negative or sad emotions. Some forms of mental illness may be associated with damage or malfunctioning of one hemisphere. Thus in schizophrenia there is some evidence of left hemisphere deficiency, but faults in connections between the hemispheres may sometimes be involved. The cerebellum is also involved with emotional conditions.

An important part of human thinking may well arise mainly, if not exclusively, in the right hemisphere. This is what might be called secret thinking—thoughts too shameful or bizarre for admission to the conscious mind. These may be sexual fantasies or suppressed sadistic reveries, for example. They go straight into the unconscious mind, and later may pop up, either naked or disguised, in dreams. Freud considered this kind of thinking so important that he called it "primary process," normal conscious thinking being relegated to the position of secondary thinking.

The term "unconscious mind" will crop up repeatedly, so a brief explanation seems necessary at this point. This is not an additional mind but a compartment, so to speak, of our whole nonmaterial mind. It is divided from the rest of the mind, i.e. the conscious mind, by a barrier which we create ourselves, though not by deliberate intention. Once a thought has passed through that barrier into the "unconscious mind," it becomes unavailable to normal memory recall. It can only be recaptured when the brain and conscious mind are still, as in reverie, meditation, or sleep, or by hypnosis.

The liaison brain (as defined by Eccles) that is linked to the conscious mind is said to be located almost wholly in the left hemisphere, which deals with concrete, logical matters. Conversely, it seems likely that the right hemisphere, which concerns itself mainly with nonverbal, nonlogical thinking, may be linked mainly with the unconscious mind, which is the source of our daydreams and our night dreams. In sleep we may suppose that the more computer-like left hemisphere is busy doing its filing, so to speak, sorting out the day's events, strengthening memory traces, and so forth. It should do this work in private, but sometimes the activity is so intense that it intrudes into consciousness and keeps us awake. Usually, however, the unconscious mind would be free to inject material from its own memory store via the right hemisphere into the dreaming consciousness. These ideas will be elaborated in Chapter 10.

Gregory Mitchell, a freelance researcher, has devised a bilateral skin-resistance meter which can be used to measure the difference in skin resistance between the two hands (Mitchell 1979). He has shown that mental activities of a kind likely to arouse the left hemisphere result in decreased skin resistance in the right (contra-lateral) hand, and vice versa. It is claimed that the instrument can be used in various ways to enhance mind development, mental ability, and fuller utilization of brain capacity.

Resumé

The two hemispheres of the brain are initially equipotent, but start to specialize in late childhood. Usually, among Westerners, the left hemisphere assumes dominance, allied to right-handedness, since the nervous systems of the two sides of the body cross over and are controlled by the opposite sides of the brain. The left hemisphere tends to deal in detail with practical matters, calculations, logic, analysis, and language. The right hemisphere is usually more holistic, abstract, and synthetic, concerned with art and music, pictures and patterns. Normally the two half-brains are closely integrated via a thick nerve bundle called the corpus callosum. Much of this knowledge derives from subjects who had this nerve bundle severed to cure severe epilepsy; but evidence of specialization in normal subjects can be obtained experimentally. Individual variations in specialization seem probable. Ideally, balanced development of the two hemispheres should be sought, thus diminishing dominance. Means by which this may be achieved are discussed.

8

Brain Rhythms

Nature has a complexity and subtlety which approaches that of the mind. I'm trying to say that we have too simple a view about nature.

David Bohm

As with knowledge of the specialization of right and left brain hemispheres, information about the electrical activity of the brain has become popularized. An electroencephalogram (EEG) can readily measure the rhythmic voltage changes that occur in many parts of the brain almost all the time, whether we are awake or asleep. The machine usually records these oscillations with a pen on a moving strip of paper, but they can be made known in other ways. For example, there are instruments that produce a light or an audible tone when the brain goes into the restful condition known as alpha rhythm; another instrument multiplies all the frequencies to bring them into the audible range, so that the familiar waves (beta, alpha, theta, and delta) produce tones ranging roughly from those of a piccolo to those of a bassoon.

The frequencies of various brain waves are as follows:

Beta rhythm   13 cycles per second upwards
Alpha rhythm   8–13 cycles per second, commonly 10
Theta rhythm   4–8 cycles per second
Delta rhythm   Up to 4 cycles per second.

Well characterized states of brain and mind activity are associated with each of these rhythms. In fact, it is better to concentrate on these states as the fundamental phenomena, since the actual frequencies may vary somewhat among individuals, as will be noted.

Beta rhythm represents the normal condition of the busy active brain, thinking and planning normal activities, for example, or ruminating deliberately about events. In this state brain and mind are clearly working in tandem.

Alpha rhythm represents a resting condition of the brain. It occurs in vacuous states as well as when one indulges deliberately in mental relaxation. This rhythm surely marks a partial dissociation of mind and brain, but more precisely a situation in which both are functioning in a *passive mode.* Sense impressions are still impinging upon the brain and are being registered and passed on to the mind. Consciousness, via the mind, is idly taking note of the impressions; it may, for instance, be hearing music inattentively in the passive mode in which we hear background music. An experienced music-lover may indeed enjoy familiar music while the brain is in alpha rhythm, but only in a noncritical, nonanalytical fashion. As soon as he pays attention to it, he slips back into beta rhythm.

Theta rhythm represents a state of reverie in which consciousness is open to the unconscious, to inspiration and intuition. I suggest that it involves more complete dissociation of mind and brain than does alpha rhythm. The brain is still in a passive state receiving sense impressions, but they are mostly ignored. The mind, however, is in an active mode, or is poised for action, but it is inward-turned, in a receptive condition, and is operating independently of the brain. This situation will be explored more fully in later chapters. It should be recalled, however, that intuitions can slip into the mind unexpectedly at odd moments; in other words, it is not necessary to assume the theta state deliberately to receive them (though it may be that when they do come in this fashion, the mind *is* momentarily in a theta state).

Some individuals get into this receptive state, during meditation for instance, while their brain rhythms are at the alpha-theta borderline of 8 cycles per second, or even showing strong waves at around 9 or 10 cycles per second, which is within the normal alpha range. Some people get drowsy and may tend to fall asleep while in the theta state; if they are deliberately attempting creative work, it may be useful for them to arrange for some slight noise to occur at intervals, to keep them quietly alert.

Delta rhythm represents a state of dormancy, just prior to or during sleep. The brain is almost completely unreceptive to sense stimuli. The mind, too, is in a similarly dormant state, and is presumably preparing to dissociate itself from the brain rather completely at the moment of sleep.

The nature of these various brain waves may be roughly illustrated in relation to driving a car. Beta rhythm corresponds to driving in traffic with maximum attention. In alpha rhythm the car is stationary, out of gear and idling. Theta rhythm corresponds to driving the car on a long straight road in high gear; the brain is in charge, functioning almost automatically, and the mind is free to think of other things. In delta rhythm the car is parked, with the engine barely running, without attention; falling asleep is represented by the moment the engine stalls.

SIGNIFICANCE OF BRAIN RHYTHMS

In the early days, a number of misconceptions arose, and exaggerated ideas on the significance and importance of brain states were rife. In particular, the alpha rhythm state of mental relaxation was hailed as a wonderful discovery. At first it was said that the alpha state happened automatically on closing the eyes. But this is not so. On the one hand it is perfectly possible to go on thinking in beta rhythm with the eyes closed; indeed many people find they can think more clearly with closed eyes, avoiding visual distraction. On the other hand, whereas opening the eyes normally reinstates beta rhythm, it is possible with practice to continue in alpha rhythm with open eyes. Probably most people slip into alpha rhythm when they close the eyes and stop active thinking.

The alpha state seems to be the starting point of various mind control systems. Doubtless such training is useful for people with restless minds, who find it difficult to switch off and cease active thinking or the "internal dialogue" in which the brain goes on mulling over the day's happenings or one's problems. The ultimate in gadgetry seems to be a machine for *inducing* alpha rhythm in both brain hemispheres. The appropriate frequency is generated electronically and fed in via small electrodes placed on the mastoid bones behind each ear. This is said to bring the brain into the relaxed alpha state almost immediately. It can be used by the subject to compel mental relaxation; also by dentists and others to calm their patients before treatment.

The keynote of the alpha state is inattention. Alpha

is usually abolished by a slight touch or a loud noise, or trying to see, even through closed eyelids, or by readying the mind for thought, even without actually formulating any idea. Naturally, doing mental arithmetic brings the mind back into its usual beta rhythm—though it is said that Einstein could do it while still registering alpha rhythm. When the brain gets tired and we become drowsy, alpha rhythm may take over while the eyes are still open. Then if we fall asleep, it continues for a while.

Some have claimed that alpha rhythm is also the key to creativity and inspiration; as previously noted, some people do indeed enter this state while the brain is producing slow alpha waves. But for most people creativity is associated with theta rhythm. It should not be supposed that the whole brain goes solidly into an appropriate frequency; more often two or three rhythms appear simultaneously, presumably coming from different areas of the brain. Researchers in this field are coming to realize the need to take readings from several areas of both hemispheres. The picture is less clearcut than was originally supposed. But the major rhythm in progress seems to be spread over much of the cortex; for example, although theta rhythm is associated with the kind of mental activity that goes on in the right hemisphere, it is not limited to that side of the brain. During active thinking, beta rhythm is predominant, but it may flicker into alpha or theta, or these may be present simultaneously. Similarly, in a relaxed state alpha is predominant but may not be maintained pure for long. As long ago as 1946, Adrian postulated some central region of our being that decided upon the direction of attention and which parts of the cortex should be set free from the alpha rhythm for the use of the mind in thinking. Occasionally, no alpha waves occur at all.

Swami Rama, an Indian well versed in meditation techniques, was wired to an EEG machine at the Menninger Foundation in 1978. He soon became aware of the mental correlates of the various brain frequencies. Two of his comments were puzzling at the time, but became clearer in the light of later understanding. He said, "Alpha is nothing; theta is noisy." As noted, the alpha state is indeed for most people one of inactivity and inattention, a resting state for the brain. The theta state gives access to the unconscious, but what emerges depends upon mood and set. In the absence of any preparation, unwanted material may be dredged up from the subconscious aspect of the mind, and this would account for the epithet "noisy." On the other hand, if the subject is well prepared, if he knows what he is hoping for in this state and is seeking and needing enlightenment, then he may bring down material from what may be called the superconscious aspect of mind.

An English colleague, who also practiced meditation, was similarly wired. It transpired that on relaxing the mind he went straight through alpha to theta. But he was disappointed to find that this state brought no inspiration, psychic experiences, or whatever! Asking for nothing, that is what he received. The theta state opens the doors, but a kind of inner receptiveness is also required in order to invite revelations. A similar condition may be induced by the drug LSD; but again, what is experienced depends on mood and set, on advance preparation, if any. Without this, it is liable to be a "bad trip," with unpleasant psychic experiences. Subjects who started off in a reverential religious mood, on the other hand, had experiences on the verge of the mystical (see Chapter 16).

It might be expected that intense neuronal activity, betokened by strong brain waves, would be associated with higher states of consciousness. But this is not so; if anything, the reverse is true. This is not surprising if, as suggested, in higher states there is a tendency for the mind to operate in partial dissociation from the brain. It is rather in everyday thinking that the brain is most active, with a flurry of beta waves of changing intensity.

For completeness, a few words may be added about the electrical activity of the brain in unconscious states. In sleep there is some chaos in EEG patterns; some go faster than normal, some slower; there are bursts of disordered activity, certainly not cessation of activity, as might be expected. New wave forms called spindle waves also appear in sleep. At an interval of a few hours, organized cerebral activity is resumed with rapid waves of low intensity. This is associated with rapid eye movements (REM) that signify that the subject is having a dream (see Chapter 12). Other EEG patterns are associated with drug-induced unconsciousness, coma, epilepsy, etc.

Résumé

The brain shows rhythmic electrical activity at all times, waking and sleeping. It has about six characteristic frequencies, but the wave forms are not all simple sine waves. During active thinking, the brain normally exhibits beta rhythm of 13 or more cycles per second. With most individuals in relaxation, it goes into alpha rhythm of 8–13 cycles per second. In a state of reverie with access to the unconscious, and sometimes with creative thinking, theta waves of 4–8 cycles per second may be exhibited. In drowsiness just prior to sleep, delta waves at up to 4 cycles per second may take over. In sleep, the frequency patterns are disordered and sharp spindle waves may occur. In dreaming sleep, the wave-pattern becomes better organized, with fast waves of low intensity. There are individual variations, and steady rhythms of a single frequency throughout the brain are rare; more often two or more patterns appear together, or flickering from one to another.

9

The Seats of Memory

There is no more wonderful and necessary function of the brain than its ability to learn and to retrieve what is learned in the memory process. For each of us the most precious activities throughout our lifetime involve the storage of experiences, which in this way are made uniquely ours in that they are available for our reenactment or recall in the memory process.

Sir John Eccles

It is astonishing that having reached nearly the end of the twentieth century we are still not sure whether memories are stored in the mind or the brain. The reductionists have no alternative to the brain, and perceiving that it appears to be equal to the task, they see no problem in relegating all memories to the brain. But Sir John Eccles, who is far from being a reductionist, also takes this line. At the opposite extreme most Eastern philosophers take for granted that memories are stored in the nonmaterial mind, and see no necessity to justify their conclusions. Rupert Sheldrake, and probably some other scientists, along with writers on the ancient wisdom, follow their lead, again without stating reasons for their views. The only writer I have come across who actually argues the case for mind memory is Michael Marsh (1985).

How can it be that two university-trained men like Eccles and Marsh reach such dramatically opposed conclusions? Fortunately, it is possible to suggest an answer to this dilemma. Many of his readers may claim that Marsh is biased in his judgment. His book is entitled *A Matter of Personal Survival,* and its whole purpose is to amass plausible evidence from all possible angles for the persistence of consciousness after death of the body. If we do indeed survive as nonmaterial entities, then we *must* retain our minds, plus access to all but the most trivial of memories, or we can have no individual continuity.

Since I do firmly believe in survival, I have to go along with Marsh and those philosophers, Western as well as Eastern, who take this line. But I am also convinced by the wealth of scientific evidence deployed by Eccles and many other scientists for the encoding of memories in the physical brain. So as mentioned earlier, I feel obliged to conclude that most memories are replicated in both mind and brain.

Marsh presumably subscribes to what I call the "telephone exchange" hypothesis of memory storage; sense impressions and experiences generally are received by the brain, catalogued, and passed on for long-term storage in the mind. The brain is supposed to retain only the telephone number, so to speak, for each memory, which it uses to recall the memory on demand. But it is difficult to see how such a recall system could operate unless the brain holds the "file copy" of the memory itself, as well as its location. In any event, if the memory were indeed transferred to the conscious mind for storage, then one might suppose that it could be conjured up again directly without requiring the intervention of the brain. But in fact we do need the brain for recall—as anyone who has suffered brain damage can confirm.

The clue to the discrepant hypotheses about the seat of memory lies in the nature of the memories that are selected for study. The experimental work on human memory derives mostly from tests on animal memory. The only kind of memory that can be examined in animals is that of action routines. Animals can be taught to perform action sequences, using "stick" or "carrot" inducements. For example, they can be trained to push or pull levers for rewards of food pellets, or to run a maze. In short they can be taught tricks. Similar methods are used to train circus animals or horses for equestrian show routines. A prosperous industry has grown up in training dolphins and whales to perform feats to amuse the children (of all ages) who flock to their pools.

Human memory can be tested similarly with action sequences, but it is more usual to test factual memory. Strings of numbers or word sequences are memorized, e.g., poems, nonsense words, or sentences. Speed and accuracy of memory can be studied and also the length of time memories are retained. Now it so happens that a computer can equally well be "taught" to memorize such data; moreover, the computer will reproduce it rather more accurately than a human subject. So it is not surprising that the psychologists and brain scientists were able to establish satisfactorily that such memories are held in the brain.

Marsh, on the other hand, elected to consider complex memories of events and experiences. These would often be elaborate "scenes" incorporating messages from several sense organs, along with their interpretation, comparison with previous memories, and analysis of the total experience. It is indeed arguable whether or not such holistic images are beyond the capacity of the brain's encoding mechanisms; they could not be stored in a computer's memory bank. So again it is not surprising that Marsh reached the conclusion he needed to support his case, namely, that such memories are stored in the mind. This conclusion does lose some of its force now that electronic video recorders can record fast-moving scenes in color, with stereophonic sound. Perhaps the sophisticated brain, with its capacity for multiple parallel processing, could after all manage this. On the other hand, it may well not be fast enough.

SEAT OF MIND MEMORIES IN THE UNCONSCIOUS

It is hard to see how such alternatives could be submitted to experimental tests, so Marsh's conclusion must remain a hypothesis. But workers in both camps have extrapolated unwarrantedly from the learning situations that interested them to the conclusions that *all* types of memory are either exclusively encoded in the brain or held only in the mind, as the case may be. Does nobody believe what seems obvious to me, namely that the memory stores are (at least partially) *duplicated* in *both* mind and brain? The only answer I can find is—well yes, a few do, but only half-heartedly. Marsh, who favors mind memory, does concede that the brain may store action programs. Eccles, who favors brain memory, perceives that the brain may sometimes come up with the wrong memory trace, or one that has become faulty. So he postulates what he calls a "recollection memory" located in the mind, acting as a kind of overseer to correct such errors. Some of his diagrams seem to imply a more extensive mind memory, and his ideas on survival also require this, but he does not elaborate.

My own hypothesis differs significantly from that of Marsh in that I suggest that mind memories are stored in the *unconscious mind*. He proposes that memories are transferred from the mind to what he calls the "inmost self." Presumably this is not the same as the unconscious mind, or he would have used that term. My ideas will be expounded after the evidence for storage of memories in the brain has been reviewed.

MEMORY TYPES

Five types of memory have been described in the scientific literature; they vary somewhat in their nature and greatly in their duration.

The *iconic memory* is pictorial and extremely brief, lasting a second or less. It may be assumed that this is available only during the instant when the mind is scanning the image on the cerebral cortex. Not everyone has this type of memory.

The *short-term memory* endures for any time up to around ten seconds. It is the sort of memory we use to hold a telephone number we have just looked up, while we dial it. It is sustained by attention and by rehearsal if necessary; it fades away and is lost when attention is withdrawn, unless there is deliberate intention to record the memory. Eccles suggests that the short-term memory is held in both brain and conscious mind (Popper and Eccles 1977). In the brain there are self reexciting chains or loops in the pattern of modular excitation. Synapses communicating via neurontransmitters may be envisaged, linking a long sequence of neurons in repeated excitations at each reinforcement.

There is some evidence for an *intermediate term memory*, starting before the short-term memory fades, peaking in a few minutes, then slowly fading in an hour or two.

The most important is the *long-term memory*, detectable about half an hour after the original event, peaking at about three hours, then fading extremely slowly, over months or years; it may endure for the rest of one's life. It was once thought that there might be "memory molecules," and some claims were made for transfer of memory in lower animals by feeding or injecting the brain or brain extracts from trained animals. It is now known positively that the long-term memory traces are indeed chemical in nature. But they do not involve specific molecules, nor is a particular memory located in one special site in the brain. What is involved is ordinary protein synthesis taking place on "modifiable synapses," changing and enlarging them.

It is reasonable to suppose that this consolidation of memory traces involves the same synapses as those taking part in the evanescent short-term memory phase. It has been shown that the chemical cycloheximide, which is known to inhibit protein synthesis, does prevent the buildup of long-term memory (in chickens). Other drugs inhibit either the short-term memory or the labile or intermediate-term memory. A long-term memory trace involving synthesis of protein in synapses is believed to meander through a considerable region of the brain. It is also known that the hippocampus, a small organ in the forebrain, is concerned in this process of memory encoding. Excision of the hippocampus from both hemispheres (to relieve bilateral epilepsy centered in these organs) was found to destroy the capacity to build up any long-term memories. The subject retained recollection of events prior to the operation, but for current events he was left with only brief memories—a most unfortunate and unexpected result of the surgery.

Eidetic memory occurs only in exceptional individuals. It takes the form of vivid, detailed pictorial memory of events. This can be called up at will, and the picture in the "mind's eye" can be scanned for details. It seems likely that such eidetic images are indeed stored in the mind, not the brain.

To complete the list, the *recognition memory* postulated by Eccles must be added.

A review in *Nature* (Goelet et al. 1986) permits some amplification of this account. Recent work, mainly on invertebrates, confirms that acquisition of long-term memories does involve gene expression and synthesis of new proteins. Acquisition of short- and intermediate-term memories does not involve synthesis of new protein, but it now appears that it does involve enzymic chemical reactions to modify existing proteins (specifically by phosphorylation). These proteins modulate the properties of nerve cells and synapses. It is also confirmed that long-term memory traces consolidate the prior more transient ones with newly synthesized protein laid down along the same paths. Problems remain; it is still not known how repetitions of training sessions initiates this consolidation into long-term memories. It is not certain that all these findings can be extrapolated to the human situation, especially since human short-term memory is accorded a shorter duration (up to ten seconds) than that of invertebrates. Later research has confirmed that laying down long-term memory traces does entail growth of synapses (Morris et al. 1986). For additional research on long-term memory traces, see the review by Mortimer Mishkin and Tim Appenzeller (Mishkin et al. 1987).

LEARNING

Understanding the ways that brain and mind function should enable us to use both more efficiently. In particular, it should assist the process of education, of learning and memorizing. It used to be thought that we came into this world as blank sheets, so to speak, upon which anything could be imprinted. This is, of course, exactly how the electronic computer works; information is fed in only once and is retained indefinitely in the memory bank, unless the mechanism develops a fault. But human memory is not like this. As the work of linguist Noam Chomsky and others suggests, we are born with innate understanding of the structure of language, for example. The infant is primed, as it were, to pick up any language it hears spoken. If the parents are bilingual, it may even learn two languages simultaneously, and during childhood it will come to understand both and to speak either fluently as the occasion requires.

We inherit other learning abilities also, and they are not like those of a computer. We are less competent than it at memorizing unrelated bits of information; we need to have these repeated several times, or to read them more than once before we can retain such lists reliably. But unlike the computer, we can learn to understand the *meaning* of information, and we remember better what we do understand. We prefer to learn by association, by relating new information to what we know already. The mind likes to arrange its intake into patterns which it then remembers readily. The numerous systems for memory training take advantage of this knowledge. Words and facts to be remembered are linked deliberately at presentation with words in common use that have some logical or specious relationship with the new information; we are given mnemonics to help us remember. The relationship may be phonetic as in Cockney slang, or there may be some structural similarity between the pairs of words, for example. It has been suggested that education could be revolutionized if teachers took full advantage of such understanding of how brain and mind are innately designed to function. Children could learn more easily; they would enjoy being taught; and they would remember their lessons better. Teachers and pupils alike would undergo less stress, and the whole education system would become more efficient.

The capacity of a trained memory can be truly prodigious. This may be illustrated in terms of music. Most people remember the songs they sang in their youth. But composers and conductors can remember entire symphonies, including the parts for every instrument in the orchestra. Moreover, they can recall specific performances of a symphony, and the way different conductors interpreted the work. The quality of musical memory is also astounding. The musically trained can distinguish closely related instruments by their timbre and range of overtones: for example oboe and clarinet; flute and recorder; violin and viola. From a recording of a piece of music heard for the first time, the contribution of each instrument can be picked out.

Various attempts have been made to classify memory in relation to contents or to modes of recovery. Episodic memory of an event holistically complete with time and place has already been distinguished from semantic memory of general information stored without relation to the original occasion of acquisition. Recognition signifies that knowledge of a particular memory is available, or, as Eccles notes, recognition that a recall has been made incorrectly. The actual retrieval of a memory is called "recall," but this can be further subdivided. Remembrance has been used to signify spontaneous recall, and recollection to mean willed recall, sometimes involving some effort. Reminiscence is different again; it involves recall, not always in precise detail, along with aesthetic appreciation of the memory and related matters.

EVIDENCE FOR DUAL MEMORY SYSTEMS

What might be called "working memories" are held in the brain, available for quick recall; the evidence for this seems quite conclusive. Why then should the issue be complicated by postulating mind memory as well?

It is indeed difficult to find direct evidence, but the indirect evidence seems highly persuasive. It can be divided into two parts. The first part follows from the belief in survival after physical death; it will be dismissed by those who believe that individual consciousness is extinguished at death. The second part depends upon analysis of normal experiences during earth life, and these should not be summarily dismissed. This book is not the place for any detailed discussion of survival (see for example Marsh 1985 and Smith 1986). I will only point out that later chapters consider exalted states of consciousness that we can enter into, at least briefly in "peak experiences"; it seems logical that we may abide in such states during the afterlife. Assuming, then, that such conditions do prevail after death, it is obvious that they must provide for access to our treasured memories. These may fade slowly as we progress to higher states of consciousness, but instant amnesia would be an unwelcome and unproductive condition.

Most people who do believe in an after-death life also believe in some kind of conscious nonphysical existence before birth. Consciousness implies the ability to think and to communicate with other entities in like condition, and to be aware of external conditions in this nonphysical world. So in such a state, we already must have minds and senses of some kind. During the prenatal stage, these later faculties have to be replicated in the form of the physical sense organs. Similarly the mind, which presumably already had the ability to remember, is replicated in the brain, which can also encode memories. Such replication is not redundant; it is a necessity for the conditions of physical life.

It may be objected that we are not born with memories of this nonmaterial world. To this there are several answers. First, the statement is not altogether true. Some children do retain intimations of an earlier existence, as Wordsworth pointed out:

> Our birth is but a sleep and a forgetting,
>   The soul that rises with us, our life's star,
> Hath elsewhere had its setting,
>   And cometh from afar.

Secondly, such memories would be in the unconscious mind, *not* accessible to ready recall. Thirdly, they would be crowded out, and soon forgotten, by the exciting new experiences of the baby in coming to terms with the physical world.

There are many experiences in normal life that can be better understood by postulating a second memory bank in the unconscious mind. It has been argued (Marsh 1985) that the brain is probably incapable of retaining complete complex memories of eventful scenes. It is perhaps more accurate to suggest that the brain can retain memories of the separate ingredients of such events, but *not* of the integrated holistic experience itself. That entire happening can only be stored in the unconscious mind. So how does this happen in the first place, and how can we recall such memories?

To explain, we may return to what is known, and what may be inferred, about the right and left brain hemispheres. In Chapter 6 we noted with some surprise that the liaison brain described by Eccles appears to be limited to an area in the cortex of the left hemisphere only. He presumed that the right hemisphere's communication with the mind could only proceed via the corpus callosum and this liaison area in the left cortex. This seems an improbable situation. If this were really the only mode of mind-brain communication, then subjects who had the corpus callosum cut, and those few who had the left hemisphere excised completely, would become severely crippled and virtually mindless, whereas in fact they appear to function almost normally after full recovery from the operation.

Mind-brain contact across an interface does indeed seem appropriate for the kind of factual information that is processed in the left hemisphere, and for the reverse traffic in motor commands. Thus for the complex events taken as our example, it is straightforward to imagine the separate components being handled by the left hemisphere and passed on to the mind via its liaison area. As noted, these items could also be encoded in brain memory. But the experience as a whole, including emotional and aesthetic overtones, is more appropriate for handling by the right hemisphere. It then seems necessary to envisage some more intimate, perhaps three-dimensional liaison mechanism whereby the holistic experience can be communicated directly from the right hemisphere to the mind. It may well be impossible to demarcate the physical structures involved in this transfer, but the etheric brain, mentioned in Chapter 6, would serve admirably as the intermediary. Such speculations pass beyond the boundaries of orthodox science into the realms of parapsychology and parabiology, but this is no reason for dismissing them out of hand.

In one sense, it is already common knowledge that some part of our memory is held in the unconscious mind. Psychologists tell us that we repress or suppress unwelcome knowledge about ourselves and other people, pushing it out of the way into the subconscious. We do not usually regard such material as memory, and indeed it is unlike most mind memories in that often it has never been fully formulated in words. Nor does it reappear readily in consciousness like other memories. It is more likely to pop up in dreams or to surface in the shape of vague fears and uneasiness. In any event, this phenomenon concerns only a small part of the hypothesis that most of our memories are duplicated in brain and unconscious mind. This hypothesis may be limited to some degree. It may be supposed that routine memories such as motor programs are left in the brain only once they have been worked out. This is somewhat analogous to operating a computer. We do not need to know how it was programmed; all we need to know is the code that instructs it to perform its numerous functions. Thus the two memory banks are not identical. There is material in the brain not present in the unconscious mind, and much in the latter that is not duplicated in the brain.

LOSS AND RECALL OF MEMORY

To appreciate why the second memory has to be assigned to the unconscious mind, it is necessary to consider not only remembering, but also forgetting, as well as the effects of brain damage, including amnesia. We all forget facts we once knew, and increasingly so in old age. In other words, we remain aware that at some time we had the missing data safely ensconced in the brain's memory bank. But now, as we say, "It escapes me." Sometimes it emerges later from oblivion.

The materialist must perforce assume that the defective memory trace in the brain has somehow become reactivated. Indeed this may be a general assumption. But it seems physically improbable, because long-term brain memory is generally believed to be chemical in nature, involving newly synthesized protein. It appears to be laid down in the form of modifications to a chain of synapses. Possibly such a chain is reinforced by additional protein synthesis when it is used frequently. When it falls into disuse, however, it is likely that the component protein breaks down again into its constituent amino acids, so that the chain is physically broken by this decomposition. Thus the memory trace no longer exists at all. It would not be reconstructed just by wishing to have it available. This could be done only by recommitting the data to memory. The loss is analogous to the degeneration of a disused muscle, which can be built up again only by exercise.

It is more plausible to suppose that when a memory does come back, it is dredged up from the unconscious mind. This hypothesis accords well with the experience of the way the recovery occurs. If the second memory remained in the conscious mind, we need never forget anything; we could command recall from either brain or mind memory. Thus if a memory trace in the brain became weak from age, lack of reinforcement, and disuse, so that accurate recall was difficult or impossible, we could instantly fall back on the second memory. We know from experience that this is not possible, at least not instantly on demand. Normally we must rely on our brain memory, but recovery from the unconscious mind is not wholly impossible; it just requires a different technique. Generally it is useless to command the lost memory to emerge. It is imperative to stop a frantic search, to still the mind, and to slip into a state of reverie, of quiet inner listening. Then soon, or sometimes much later when we are otherwise engaged, and without warning, the missing word slips into the mind in a flash, with the "Eureka" impact of an intuition. Sometimes it comes piecemeal; a clue may jog the memory or a friend may offer a helpful suggestion. Then a little later it comes complete: "Got it! It's helychrisum." If the memory persistently refuses to emerge, the quest must be postponed. After an interval, we may *gently* interrogate the memory store, asking if the information is available yet. Sometimes the answer appears at once in the mind; at other times it is still unavailable but may come up still later.

Let me reaffirm that for me such an experience is completely different from normal recall of brain memories. For example, I may need to address an envelope, and the names and numbers flow smoothly into my mind as I write, without effort or surprise. If I forget, say, the zip code, then I do not waste time searching the second memory; I just look it up in the address book. Similarly, I may be repeating silently the form of words I use in meditation, and they come to me as required. But sometimes I make a slip or get the words in the wrong order. I know immediately that something is wrong (recognition memory?), so I just back up a bit, and this time the right words flow. The mind tells me of the error, but the words come from the brain memory. In creative writing, on the other hand, the situation again resembles the interrogation of the unconscious mind for lost memories, though not exactly the same. Then one induces a mood of openness to the unconscious mind, or rather to the superconscious mind, whence inspiration comes. This topic will be discussed in Chapters 11 and 14.

It may happen that we pass someone in the street who looks familiar. Then we remember that we met just once, about ten years ago at a party. But we chide ourselves because we have forgotten her name! In such situations we fail fully to appreciate the wonder of the human brain and our dependence upon it; we may continue to do so until we come to know someone who has suffered severe brain damage, perhaps from a stroke. This may have arisen from the bursting of a blood vessel in one hemisphere, leading to paralysis of the opposite side of the body, slurring of speech, and extensive loss of memory. The subject may recover fully from the paralysis as other parts of the brain take over from the damaged section. He may similarly regain control of the vocal apparatus, but it remains painful to listen as he stumbles over his sentences, unable to find the right words to express his thoughts, repeatedly making fresh starts using words that are still available. Memory for past events may be fairly clear, but expressing them fluently can remain impossible for years. Once again, we must conclude that the second memory is not in the conscious mind, since if it were it would be freely accessible to supplement the damaged brain memory. Moreover, recovery from the unconscious mind is inhibited by the subject's irritation and frustration at his disabilities. The condition may slowly improve as the accessible brain memories are rebuilt, either by transfer from the unconscious mind in quiet moments or by relearning from other sources.

Concussion is another situation that causes loss of memory. A blow to the head, severe enough to induce brief or prolonged unconsciousness, results in destruction of short-term and intermediate-term memories. That is to say, it is impossible to recall the event itself and whatever happened during the previous hour, approximately. This is understandable on the basis that these shorter, temporary memories circulate in loops of neurons and synapses. It may be supposed that severe shaking of the relatively gel-like brain contents washes away the neurotransmitters between synapses, and so destroys the tenuous memory circuits. The long-term memory might well have been laid down later *along the same paths*, being consolidated by relatively slow protein synthesis. But when concussion intervenes, the circuit is instantly disrupted before this consolidation can occur. There is of course no memory of the period of unconsciousness. Moreover, return of consciousness may be gradual, like awakening from a deep sleep but more prolonged. The mind (actually the brain) may be sluggish and confused for hours (I write from personal experience). It is said that the lost memories may return gradually; in my own case, they have not reappeared during some sixty years, so presumably they are permanently lost.

When recall does occur, this has intriguing implications. It must represent recall of memories that were *never laid down* in long-term synaptic pathways. Thus the memories never existed in the brain in enduring form; one would expect that recall can *only* arise from the second memory in the unconscious mind, as postulated for other forgotten material.

I submit that all these considerations, taken together, fully justify the postulation of a dual memory system encoded in both the brain and the unconscious mind.

RÉSUMÉ

There is good evidence that both short-term and long-term memories are held in the brain. The laying down of long-term memory appears to involve protein synthesis in a chain of synapses meandering through the brain and not locatable in a particular area. In addition, there is good reason to postulate a second memory, held in the mind and specifically in the unconscious mind. This type of memory holds in particular holistic records of complex events involving multiple sense impressions; it may even be doubted if the brain is adequate to store such involved memories. Meaningful survival after death necessitates a mind memory. It is probably assimilated via the right brain hemisphere. Unlike brain memory, this second memory is not accessible to instant recall on demand; retrieval may occur when the mind is in a relaxed state of reverie, often associated with theta brain rhythm. Unlike a computer, the brain prefers to associate new facts with existing knowledge. Implications of such understanding of brain and mind functions for teaching are discussed. The enormous capacity and discrimination of a trained memory is illustrated in relation to music. The effects of concussion and brain damage upon memory are discussed.

10

Brain Thinking, Emotional Thinking, Mind Thinking

Imagination is more important than knowledge.
Einstein

Some common sayings can throw light upon our modes of thinking. Some, on the other hand, are positively misleading. One, which must have been coined by someone with a lazy mind, proclaims, "You cannot think of two things at once." But of course you can, and you frequently do. For example, you may be driving a car, listening to the radio or a cassette, and conversing with one or more passengers, all at the same time. This may be unwise, but it is certainly quite common practice.

There is, however, some truth in the saying if it implies the impossibility of paying *full* attention to two lines of thought simultaneously. If two different matters of concern are "on your mind" at the same time, it is indeed likely that attention flickers from one to the other and back. At one particular instant attention is directed to only one of them; the other is "in the back of the mind," clamoring for attention, which it soon receives, reversing the situation briefly. In any event, it is certainly possible to pay *partial* attention to a number of things simultaneously—up to seven items, it has been claimed.

Contrariwise, it is possible to discriminate totally between numerous items presenting themselves for consideration. The "cocktail party phenomenon" may be given as an example. At such a party, there is usually a babel of conversation and other noise; yet it is entirely possible to dismiss all of this except the words of one person with whom you wish to converse. This rather remarkable ability is sometimes called the "filter phenomenon." However, in this situation, if someone calls your name from across the room, this one item will bypass the filter and engage your attention.

In all such situations, it is clear that mind and brain are working closely in tandem. But in other circumstances, it is possible for the brain to work alone, as noted in Chapters 4 and 5. Sense impressions are registered by the brain and presented for consideration; but if we are not interested, we may ignore them. Similarly, action programs, such as those controlling walking, are operated by the brain alone without intervention by the mind; indeed if the mind *is* directed to the performance, one is liable to stumble! This can be particularly disastrous when one has a momentary fear of being unable to cope with an unfamiliar flight of stairs; unnecessary interference by the mind can well be the cause of an accident. For purposive thinking, however, mind and brain are indissolubly linked throughout life; only at death is this link permanently severed.

BRAIN-MIND DISSOCIATION

Thus in everyday thinking, mind and brain are both involved, working in cooperation, though their respective contributions may vary greatly. In some circumstances the brain is the senior partner, operating almost without reference to the mind; conversely, in deep meditation the brain is quiescent, the mind functioning almost wholly unfettered. In separative states (out-of-body experiences, dreaming, etc.) dissociation is again almost complete, but the brain is presumably minimally involved since such experiences are sometimes recalled on return to the physical body.

It is also important to note that mind and brain can be simultaneously engaged in quite different lines of thinking. The performance of unrelated mental activities while driving a car is an example already cited. Again, as noted in Chapter 4, the brain may be busy garnering, analyzing, and interpreting sense impressions, while the mind is equally busy with something quite different, taking no notice of what the brain is doing on its own account. Similarly, the mind may be active in other ways while the brain organizes complex motor programs by itself.

It might almost be said that hands, arms, feet, and legs have subsidiary brains of their own, as also does the eye. Organs such as the heart, lungs, stomach again seem to have their own mini-brains, in the form of nerve plexuses linked to the brain itself by long axons. Indeed, it can be said that the entire physical body including the brain has a primitive consciousness in its own right. It looks after us efficiently when we walk about daydreaming and not paying proper attention to where we are going. When we get stiff in bed or lie awkwardly, impeding the blood flow to a limb, it turns us over without waking us up. But it *does* wake us up if danger seems to threaten and when it is time to get up.

HIGHER MIND AND LOWER MIND

In the opening chapters we have considered the numerous anatomical and functional subdivisions of the physical brain. Now we must turn to the more subtle, less rigid subdivisions of the nonmaterial mind. It might be said, in a rather crude analogical sense, that the mind is divided both "vertically" and "horizontally." The "vertical" division, into conscious and unconscious mind, has necessarily been mentioned in relation to memory (Chapter 9). This will be considered in greater depth in later chapters. We are presently obliged to face the more fundamental "horizontal" division into lower mind and higher mind.

In ancient Indian psychologies, mind (manas) is divided rather sharply into these two divisions, lower mind and higher mind, the abode respectively of the lower self or personality and of the higher self or real self. The lower mind is strongly linked with the emotional or desire nature (kama); the complex is called kama-manas in Sanskrit. In many instances, and especially in less developed peoples, the leading partner is kama or desire rather than mind. The personality is said to be driven by kama. Correspondingly, the higher mind is linked to a superior principle called buddhi, the realm of abstract love and wisdom. So the Indian psychologies speak of buddhi-manas as the characteristic of the higher self, from which come the messages of conscience, intuition, and inspiration. In some systems three divisions of mind are postulated. The additional one is the bridge between higher and lower mind, a realm of pure thinking not influenced by either kama or buddhi.

These divisions and associations have only rather recently become recongized in Western psychologies, even though they are relatively easy to appreciate introspectively. In this book these situations are accepted. Moreover, it is suggested that in lower-mind-emotional thinking, mind and brain are working closely together. In higher-mind-intuitional thinking, on the other hand, the mind is probably working largely on its own, and the lower mind and brain are involved subsequently, to formulate and consolidate conclusions and to record them in memory.

EMOTIONAL LINKS WITH LOWER MIND

Much commonplace thinking is obviously associated with our desires, wants, and needs—accommodation, clothes, food, career, hopes, fears, ambitions, friends, enemies, relatives, sex, and so forth. Emotions and thought are both involved in all such activities, sometimes one being dominant, sometimes the other. The most intense and purest emotions are still accompanied by thought. Conversely even the purest thinking, say solving a mathematical problem, includes overtones of emotion, such as the desire to succeed in the exercise.

In Western psychology, emotion and thought tend to be treated separately. In his book *The Human Psyche* Eccles includes a chapter entitled "The Emotional Mind," but it is concerned mainly with the relation between affects (pleasant and unpleasant sense impressions), and the way they are handled by the limbic system. There is little about the relation between thought and emotion.

In recent years however, a "new" theory has been pioneered by William Gray, a psychiatrist at Newton Center, Massachusetts (Gray 1982). He affirms that feelings and emotions, not thoughts, are the primary driving force in our lives. Thoughts are, as it were, carried along on the tide of emotions. This theory represents basically a rediscovery of the ancient Indian system, though Gray has developed it further and has perhaps taken it somewhat beyond what is reasonable. We pride ourselves on being intellectual persons, not swayed by emotions, but in fact the reverse is true, according to Gray, whose ideas are supported by systems theorist Paul

La Violette and by research at the University of Massachusetts. It is claimed that we rarely experience simple primary emotions. Instead we feel a range of emotions, differentiated and blended in different proportions for each thought. Gray calls these nuances of feeling. All thoughts and memories are held to be coded by subtle feeling tones accompanying perception. Our thoughts tend to be initiated by our desire nature and to float along on a sea of emotions. Feelings are prior to thought in evolutionary sequence, and they remain primary still; they engender thought as a secondary phenomenon. We are more intelligent than animals because we first developed a richer emotional life than they enjoy, declares Gray. In later times the balance has swung the other way, and we have tended to become excessively intellectual. So we tend to suppress, ignore, and deny the emotional-feeling nature which energizes our thoughts. We should be happier and better integrated individuals if we recognized and accepted the true state of affairs.

In understanding, learning, and remembering situations there are—or there should be—powerful emotional components. We understand other people far better when we like them, better still when we love them. It is common knowledge that children learn subjects more easily and quickly when they like them, when they are interested in them, or when they are taught in an interesting fashion by sympathetic teachers. Contrariwise, subjects that are presented merely as conjunctions of dull facts, in a purely cerebral fashion, are much harder to absorb and do not hold the pupil's attention. This kind of situation persists into adult life; it is not just a characteristic of irresponsible children who refuse to learn their lessons. Emotional involvement is a great help if we wish to study anything, at any age.

Confirmation of these ideas comes from a study on the use of computers for teaching children. Initially, while the children were interested and excited by the idea of getting information from computers, they paid more attention and learned more quickly. But they soon became bored with the soulless and totally unemotional machines, and fell back to around the same level as comparable groups taught throughout by live teachers. This is not to say that computers are useless in schools. When pupils actively operate them, even just to play computer games, this sharpens their wits. When they learn to write their own programs, they are really getting somewhere; they are starting to become creative thinkers. When the feeling side is ignored, whether unavoidably by passive use of computers or by overintellectual teachers pressed for time, then efficiency and speed of learning is impaired. There are no effective shortcuts in the education process. Learning tends to be slow and shallow when it is pursued along purely cognitive lines. It may seem a waste of time for a teacher to inject some emotional interest into otherwise dull facts, but this approach is far more effective in the long run. Such ideas are emphasized in a recent review by Nicholas Maxwell, which suggests that education to develop *wisdom* is needed to solve global problems (Maxwell 1987).

Gray goes as far as to claim that memory encodes primarily the "feeling nuances" that accompany our thoughts, the latter being carried along as passengers, so to speak. Also, in recall it is the feeling component that first emerges from the memory bank, bringing the thoughts with it. This may well be so with emotional individuals, but I doubt if it is universally true. However, heart and mind working together form a formidable alliance. Thinking becomes more powerful, more penetrating, more effective when its guidance by feeling is not only acknowledged but is consciously taken into account and utilized in one's work. In addition, the heart-mind alliance holds the key to spiritual experience and development. We may recall the injunction of the Mexican Indian "sorcerer" don Juan to his pupil Carlos Castaneda to "put heart into your work." It is advice that might well be followed by philosophers and by scientists, particularly in the life sciences.

In complete contrast to the ideas of Gray and La Violette is the philosophy of Ayn Rand (Gray 1982). She claimed that total objectivism is the proper goal. Reasoning should be freed from all subjective influences such as feelings and emotions. One should accept total responsibility for oneself, and oneself alone on a wholly rational basis. Rand denied any suggestions that feelings might sometimes be closer to reality than logical thinking, or that the unconscious mind might ever know better than the conscious mind. Nathaniel Branden was at one time an ardent exponent of Rand's philosophy, but later broke away when he saw the results of her teachings on young people not yet fully mature. They became ardent and self-righteous suppressers of the emotional side of life; they experienced guilt and self-alienation. Branden came to see the need for a balance between thought and emotion, and perceived that intense feelings can lead to true creative thinking.

MIND THINKING

Beyond the relatively automatic brain thinking and commonplace lower mind thinking about intimate personal concerns—which is highly tinged by emotions if not controlled thereby—lies a more refined mode of thinking. It is relatively impersonal in character and includes thoughts on ultimate abstract principles, ethics, religion, global government, art, science. In this mode we seem to have largely shaken loose from both brain and emotions, so that this might be termed pure mind thinking. Such thoughts originate in the mind and are dwelt upon at that level; insofar as the brain is involved, it is as a subsidiary partner in the enterprise, not as an equal or even superior partner as in commonplace thinking. By introspection we can clearly differentiate these two modes of thinking and appreciate their respective characteristics; these are suggested in the table below.

In comparison with brain thinking, mind thinking is:

less crisp and clear-cut	more diffuse
less precise and specific	more general and vague
less deliberate and important-seeming	more receptive
less self-directed	more willing to accept direction
less earnest and urgent	more relaxed
less outward-turned	more inward-turned
less personal	more transpersonal

Creative thinkers and planners, and people who meditate regularly will readily recognize this more exalted mode, in which the frenzied everyday world is transcended temporarily. In this state one is more relaxed yet more intense and more one-pointed.

It may be noted that the characteristics of thinking with the mind alone are uncannily similar to those mental activities that are believed to occur mainly in the right hemisphere of the brain. We may reasonably assume that when thoughts of this kind are transmitted to the brain for storage in its memory bank, it is the right hemisphere that handles the traffic. Moreover, such thoughts are of the kind that are held in the unconscious mind memory as suggested in the previous chapter.

Another pointer to mind-brain dissociation is the fact that in this exalted mode it is more difficult to recall words learned by rote, a meditation for example. The mind is somewhat irked by the task, and would prefer to recall instead a corresponding sequence of pure ideas or imagined pictures or symbols not formulated in words. If we try this however, we perceive that the "pure ideas" tend to be vague and woolly, lacking the precision provided by the brain and well-selected words. We shall miss our brains when we are deprived of them at death!

It should be noted that abstract thinking is a uniquely human accomplishment. It is far beyond the scope of the most gifted of primates who have learned the elements of language, whether sign language or the use of painted symbols. Analysis by Buehler, extended by Popper, reveals that there are four levels of language. These are, starting from the simplest:

1) The expressive function by which the feelings and emotions are conveyed by cries, bird song, and so forth.
2) The signal function, which includes alarm calls by birds or mammals, gestures, facial expressions, and the like.
3) The descriptive function, which is the major part of human language. It includes all our descriptions of events and personal experiences, our political and cultural views, etc., making up the bulk of our conversation and letter-writing. This function also includes discrimination between truth and falsehood, fact and fiction, and the deliberate choice of lying when this is judged expedient.
4) The argumentative function, which encompasses higher levels of reasoning such as rational and critical thinking.

It seems evident to me that the four levels of language evolved in this order, and the fact is exemplified in the development of every child who recapitulates them one by one from babyhood to adult life. Of course, we do not outgrow the earlier levels; they permeate and enrich the later ones. Animals seem to have command of only the first two levels, despite the painstaking efforts of some researchers to prove otherwise. The chimpanzees who have laboriously mastered elementary language may string together two or three signs or symbols, but they cannot rival a child's use of syntax—which is demonstrated by a toddler as early as three years of age.

Moreover, it seems evident to me that these experiments on primates should not be regarded as being typical of the species. They relate only to individual highly domesticated animals that have been to some extent "humanized" by their devoted teachers. It is possible that their accurate responses are due to slight unconscious overt signals made by their attendants (the "clever Hans effect," named after the horse that "learned to count" in this fashion). However, it should also be recalled that a strong rapport exists between the animal and its keeper, such that telepathy may well explain the phenomenon, at least in part. Anyone who has made a close friend of an intelligent dog or cat must recognize the two-way telepathy that links them—unless they totally reject even the possibility of telepathic communication. Dolphins are also exceptionally intelligent animals. Some people believe that dolphins, and possibly whales also, have solved the language problem independently of man, by their complex "songs."

INTUITIONAL THINKING

Just as the lower mind is shot through with and energized by our feeling-emotional-desire nature, so is the higher mind infused and energized by a superior principle inherent in the human psyche. It lies beyond the mind, yet ordinarily we experience only its interaction with the higher mind. In Sanskrit it is called *buddhi*. From our more familiar levels of consciousness, we can form no clear concept of this sublime principle; we may say that it embodies spiritual love and wisdom, but we may sense vaguely that it is much more than these. Our desire nature is, so to speak, its coarse, earthy reflection.

It is from this buddhic level that we receive our higher intuitions and spiritual intimations, such as faith in a benevolent Supreme Being or some impersonal Source that envelopes and guides us. These topics will be expanded in later chapters. This state corresponds with what has sometimes been termed the "superconscious." Reductionists must perforce deny this level utterly. Contrariwise, those familiar with it may affirm from their own experience that it is closer to Reality than any other state of consciousness they know.

MENTAL ILLNESS

The entire thinking equipment is so complex that parts of it are bound to go wrong at times. Mental illnesses are indeed prevalent, especially in cities where life tends to be hectic. But the brain, despite its enormous complexity, seems to recover well from minor hiccups, thanks to built-in redundancies and self-repair mechanisms. This book has concentrated deliberately on the positive aspects of the thinking process, so it has no chapter specifically on disordered thinking. Various kinds of malfunction have been mentioned where relevant in other chapters.

At this point it is perhaps worth noting that mental illnesses can be related to specific parts of the whole subjective apparatus: to body, to brain, to etheric brain, to emotions, and to mind including its unconscious part.

Some mental illnesses originating in the body are genetically determined. For example, phenylketonuria is an inborn error of metabolism involving inability to metabolize completely the protein constituent phenylalanine. The resulting ketone compounds poison the brain and disable it. If recognized early enough, the disease can be treated with special diets, avoiding all proteins that contain significant amounts of the amino acid phenylalanine. Prenatal traumas, like German measles in the mother, can lead to brain damage in the fetus. A stroke, a bursting of a blood vessel in the brain usually due to excessive blood pressure, can result in extensive brain damage, with contralateral paralysis and difficulty with speech and memory recall (Chapter 9). These troubles may be partially cured by encouraging the brain to find alternative pathways. The brain can develop serious disorders like epilepsy, as noted in Chapter 7; this has been treated by drastic surgery.

Otherwise, most disorders arising in the brain do so in old age, leading to general slowing down of brain functions, partial loss of memory, especially short-term memory, and eventually in some subjects, senile dementia, or Altzheimer's disease. Not usually recognized as such are disorders of the etheric brain (Chapter 6). This serves not only as an intermediary between brain and mind, but also as a screen protecting us from premature objective awareness of the psychic realms. This screen or web is damaged by unwise meditative or ritualistic practices, or by excessive use of drugs and alcohol. Such abuses can lead to terrifying visions from the lower astral regions, e.g. a "bad trip" on LSD, which may cause madness in an unstable individual.

Many mental illnesses, of various varieties, arise in the mind when it is excessively influenced by powerful negative emotions, though there is increasing evidence that physical abnormalities are involved. Psychiatrists may be unable to cure or alleviate the results of such disordered thinking.

RÉSUMÉ

Contrary to the popular saying, we *can* think of several things at once. In most situations mind and brain work together in close integration, but either can function independently of the other. They can think of *different* things simultaneously. Thus if we take a walk the brain can attend to the necessary motor functions in leg muscles, while the mind enjoys the scenery or dwells on other matters. The mind is subdivided. The lower mind, the seat of the personal self, is strongly linked with the emotional nature. The higher mind, the seat of the higher self or individuality, is similarly linked to the buddhic principle, the source of inspiration. Feelings and emotions are the driving force of mundane thinking. In relatively impersonal thinking about abstract principles, the mind operates largely independently of the brain. When such thoughts are conveyed to the brain for storage in memory, then probably the right hemisphere is involved. Disordered thinking causing mental illness can arise at various levels, body, brain, etheric brain, and emotions, as well as in the mind itself.

11

Levels of Consciousness

Know atma *as the ruler of [or man in] the chariot, the body as the chariot itself; know wisdom* (buddhi) *as the charioteer, and* manas *as the reins. The senses are the horses, objects of sense are the range of action of the horses, and experience is the junction of* atma, *sense, and* manas.

Katha Upanishad

Before creative thinking and disciplined thinking can be discussed constructively, it seems necessary to seek clearer understanding of the unconscious mind, and also of the distinct levels of consciousness at which we operate. We are all familiar in subjective experience with the lowest levels—physical, emotional or astral, and mental. Beyond these, as described later in this chapter, lie the unfamiliar levels still usually known by the Sanskrit words *buddhi* and *atma*. These too can become accessible to human consciousness in exalted states.

These levels can be tabulated, or they can be represented in diagrams of various forms. All representations are misleading to some degree, for they unavoidably imply spatial separation. This impression is sometimes countered by saying that the levels all overlap, occupying the *same* space. But this notion is also misleading because the nonphysical levels are not confined to physical space with its three geometrical dimensions. Some writers have attempted to circumvent this difficulty by postulating higher dimensions, a fourth for the emotional level, a fifth for the mental level, and so forth. Hinton (1976) and some others took this scheme so literally as to regard these as *geometrical* dimensions, stretching out from a point in space in some new "within" dimension at right angles to all three dimensions of physical space.

In the later writings the new dimensions have been deprived of geometrical significance and are regarded as hypothetical or figurative, in line with the higher dimensions postulated by modern physicists. Edward Gardner (1987) introduced a novel approach by suggesting that at the emotional or astral level we do not experience an *additional* fourth dimension, but on the contrary we *lose* one dimension, absorbing it, or gaining the freedom of one geometrical dimension. We then seem to be present everywhere at once along one direction—a kind of one-dimensional omnipresence. This can of course be any particular direction we select; we then remain conscious of up and down, and of right and left, but not of forwards and backwards. This notion accounts neatly for the strange disorientation we experience in dreams and out-of-body experiences, in which we have freedom to "travel" almost instantaneously, to "see" objects from both sides at once, and so on.

Correspondingly, Gardner suggests that at the mental level we do not gain an extra fifth dimension, but the freedom of two dimensions. At the buddhic level we lose awareness of all three geometrical dimensions (or gain the freedom of all three), and we experience omnipresence in a dimensionless realm. So Gardner's scheme deals neatly with what has been postulated, or claimed by some from experience, namely that at the highest levels of consciousness accessible to us there is no sense of space or time. At these levels, consciousness is free of any spatial constraints; also past, present, and future are merged into the Eternal Now (see Chapter 16).

Contrariwise, in normal consciousness we are obsessed by space and time. When we seek to escape in some degree from such constraints, we are obliged to imagine a *direction* for the escape route. Two are commonly used; we may "rise above" our normal earthbound state, or we may retreat "within" to discover the "higher" or "inner" nature. Thus the five levels mentioned above are displayed in many theosophical or philosophical books as a tabulation or diagram with the increasingly spiritual realms appearing above the "lower" ones. If we use instead the "within" direction, the diagram can be one of concentric circles, with spirit, the Source, the Absolute, or whatever term we use for the Unimaginable, at the center. Thus the physical world appears at the circumference, which conveys a certain "rightness" since we live on the skin of our globe. Yet even this is false, like any diagram, inasmuch as we do not at all regard the inner realms as being in the interior of the earth! If this seeming implication bothers us, then we can follow Jung by turning the circle inside out; thus we illustrate a different symbolism in which we look outwards in all directions from our physical body and world, from our ignoble selves, towards greater realities beyond our normal reach.

DIAGRAMATIC REPRESENTATIONS OF LEVELS OF CONSCIOUSNESS

One of the earliest outlines of these levels must be the passage from the Katha Upanishad which stands at the head of this chapter. Various tabulations are given: in H. P. Blavatsky's *The Secret Doctrine*, in later theosophical books, in other works such as *Beyond Biofeedback* by E. and A. Green (1978) and *The Spectrum of Consciousness* and *The Atman Project* by Ken Wilber (1977 and 1978). In the present book two diagrams are offered. The first is a modified form of the tabular one, depicting the levels in horizontal layers. The second is the first

Levels of Consciousness

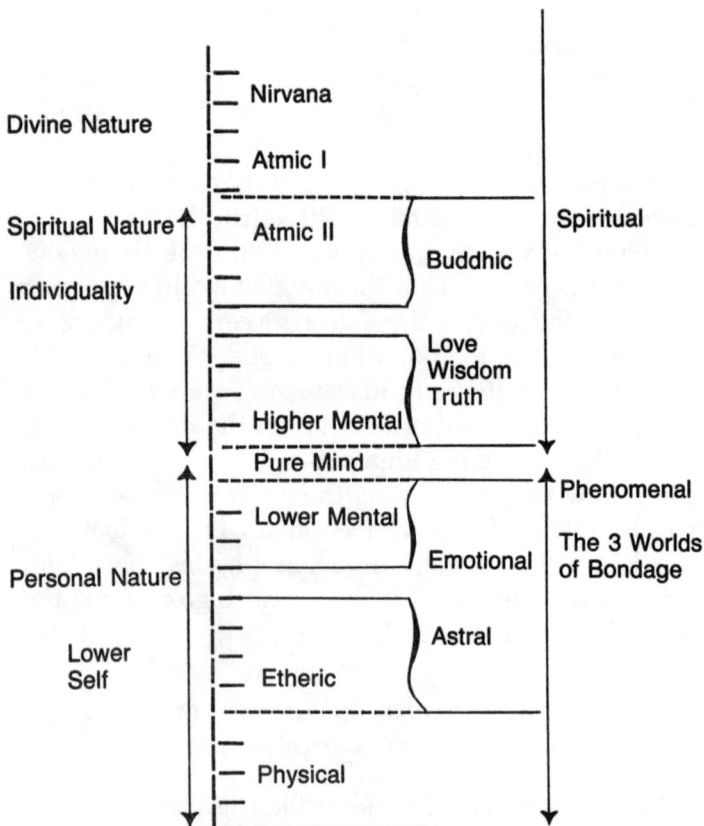

Diagram 1

States of Consciousness

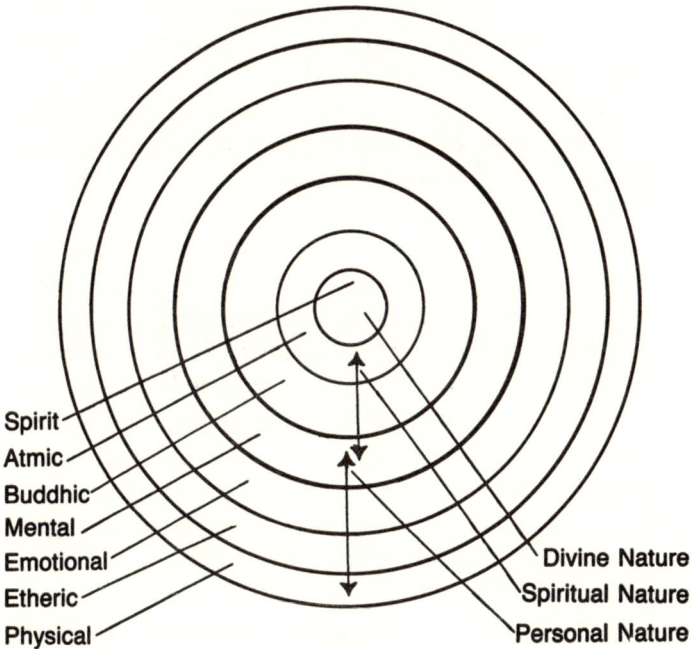

Diagram 2

type of circular diagram, with the physical world outermost.

In the tabular type of diagram, it is usual to depict the levels of consciousness one above the other in regular sequence. This arrangement conceals a rarely recognized situation, namely that the levels fall into two distinct categories. The familiar physical world is characterized by form and structure. The mental world is similar: logical thought and language are also formal and structured. Moreover, clairvoyants have described thought forms of "mental substance," persisting briefly or for longer periods. These two levels might therefore be described as feminine or form worlds. Between these two lies the emotional-feeling (astral) level, which seems to be far less organized, more flowing and vital in quality. It might accordingly be regarded as a masculine or life world. We have already noted in Chapter 10 that concrete thinking is intricately linked with emotions. Thus it may be better to regard these levels as overlapping and interacting rather than separate.

It may also be noted that the form levels are rather sharply bisected. The mental is divided into lower and higher mind, the physical into the familiar dense physical and the less well-recognized etheric. In diagram 1, accordingly, the emotional-feeling level is shown as *straddling* the lower mental and etheric levels; it is, so to speak, the life-blood of the lower mental and etheric levels. But in deference to the more usual representation, its middle segment is shown as separating these two levels. This entire arrangement is repeated at higher levels. Thus the buddhic or intuitional level, the realm of spiritual love and union, is another masculine or life world. Accordingly, it is shown as *straddling* two levels, the higher mental and part of the atmic level above, yet also separating them by its middle segment. So, repeating the lower arrangement, the buddhic may be regarded as the life-blood of these two levels.

The highest level is the Nirvana of the Buddhist, the atmic level of will or resolution, beyond the reach of all except the saints and sages among us. Most of us know it only in its aspect of will. This is not to be confused with the fickle wilfulness of half-hearted intention. It is will of a steady, silent, abiding quality, better named as resolution.

The scheme of overlapping levels was presented briefly by E. L. Gardner, but was elaborated in study groups and in his later book *The Imperishable Body* (Gardner 1948). I must take personal responsibility for the minor modification depicted in Diagram 1. However, I do not want to present the scheme authoritatively. I believe any reader who is prepared to devote enough thought to it can know these various levels of consciousness from his own experience. In the literature, such schemes are sometimes said to represent human principles, worlds or "planes," or "bodies." The one presented here is intended purely as a psychological analysis of levels as perceived in waking consciousness.

No apology is offered for introducing this complex scheme, because all its levels pertain to thinking, in its numerous modes. All are involved, from the physical and etheric brains to the resolution needed for sustained disciplined and creative thinking (see following chapters). Every level, even a half-level, has its own unique qualities, discernible by introspection. The system is not hypothetical. It has been scientifically established by repeated observation and experiment, though not wholly by the methods to which orthodox Western science arbitrarily restricts itself. (See Chapter 4, later in this chapter, and subsequent chapters.)

The etheric body, or etheric double as it is sometimes called, raises few problems. It is in effect part of the physical body, and is never fully separated until some time after death, when it is sometimes seen by a sensitive as a "churchyard ghost." The etheric is said to be the vehicle of prana or vitality. An event in my college days made me sharply aware of the reality of prana. I went with a fellow student to a lecture at another college on the current state of atomic theory. The lecture theater was full beyond capacity, and we had to stand at the back. It became very hot and stuffy, but this did not bother me; I was intent on the lecture. My companion, however, a big husky fellow, felt faint, and he put his hand on my shoulder for support. At once I felt my vitality draining away, as if sucked out by a vampire, and it was I, not he, who fainted!

The personal nature, the "lower self" or working self, resides in the physical body but extends to the etheric, emotional, and lower mental levels. It is the outpost through which we interact with the world about us, as detailed in earlier chapters. It is indispensable but it has a life of its own, and it tends to usurp authority, to run our lives for us according to its own needs and desires. The personality, moreover, is not one but many. It puts on a range of masks or persona as circumstances change. We "present a different face" to our marriage partner and friends, to shop assistants, to our employer, to those in authority. To some extent we all act out one or another of our subpersonalities, as if performing a play; to this extent we are all multiple personalities. But this term is usually reserved for individuals in whom this situation gets out of hand, as in Stevenson's famous story of Dr. Jekyll and Mr. Hyde. For a review of recent work in this field see *Brain-Mind Bulletins* (1982, 1983, 1985).

At a "higher" or "inner" level, beyond the scope of everyday mundane experience, lies the spiritual nature, the "higher self" or individuality. This embraces the higher mind, illumined by the light of buddhi, the level of spiritual love, wisdom, and truth. We enter it in moments of exaltation and intuitive awareness. This spiritual nature ought to be in effective charge of our lives, but all too often it is not. It is the voice of conscience—or it ought to be; frequently what we regard as conscience is no more than the recollection of the formal ethical code accepted by our particular civilization, rather than any inner spiritual promptings. Finally comes the atmic level of will, known only in deep mystical experience or in moments of high resolution.

It is clear from the terms employed that some conflict is implied between the "lower" and "higher" divisions of our human propensities. The terminology can usefully be clarified at this point. The loftier part has been called the "higher self," the spiritual self, the transpersonal self, or the individuality. But all these terms are unsatisfactory in one way or another. The word "self" is so closely associated with mundane selfish living that it seems inappropriate to employ it with a totally different connotation in relation to spiritual propensities, the characteristics of which are *unself*ishness and *selfless*ness. Moreover the use of "Self" (with a capital S) for the Supreme seems even less appropriate. To avoid such difficulties, in the diagrams the terms "personal nature," "spiritual nature," and "divine nature" are used. The term "individuality" is sometimes used for the spiritual nature, in contrast to "personality." This again is not wholly satisfactory. As noted in Chapter 16, it is more appropriately used in the form "sense of individuality" to denote the level at which consciousness is mainly focused at a particular time; for this is where the individual I-ness is functioning. For example if one perceives oneself to be centered in the spiritual nature, then the divine nature appears to be "above" and the personal nature "below," and both are temporarily out of focus. Sooner or later, in life or after death, a battle for supremacy has to be fought out between the personal nature and the spiritual nature. This conflict is mentioned in the New Testament, especially by St. Paul, and it forms part of Christian theology. It also appears somewhat hazily in the psychologies of Freud, Jung, and others. The nature of the conflict, its causes and mode of resolution, are set out more clearly in Buddhism. Resolution of this conflict is one of the early stages of yoga practice, particularly in Raja Yoga. It is this battle that is depicted allegorically in *The Bhagavad Gita*.

Unity within Diversity

The diagram within a circle or sphere has another significance which is vital to our discussion. The whole of creation, with its inner and outer realms, is depicted within one globe. This suggests, and is meant to suggest, that in a certain sense the manifest universe is encompassed within a single unity. All is one, not only in some vague religious or hypothetical sense, but in an intensely real sense, that can be vividly known for oneself in the mystical experience. A single such experience of "self-evident truth" can so enrich the remainder of one's life that one can never again feel separate and lonely, even when one is physically alone. This theme of unity latent in diversity is not only central to oriental philosophies, but has been expounded in the West in recent decades. In respect to humanity, the theme has become known as transpersonal psychology, notably in America, and most notably espoused by Ken Wilber. We are faced with a paradox between our everyday experience of diversity and intimations of unity. It can be resolved intellectually to some extent, especially by anyone whose heart is filled with love, but it can only be fully absorbed and comprehended in the mystical state.

Descending somewhat from these lofty heights of unshakable certainty, it is necessary to use a spate of words to expound this additional significance in our diagram. The center represents unconditional unity or oneness. Proceeding outwards, diversity and individuality intrude, at first hardly noticed, but becoming increasingly evident, till at the physical level we are flung apart as separate beings, as if by the centrifugal force of our spinning globe. At this level, it takes a deliberate exercise of imagination to believe that we are not really intrinsically independent entities. The higher mental-buddhic realm is roughly that at which we experience unity yet still recognize our individuality, or at least we know that we shall revert to that stage when the mystical experience ends. The main objective of yoga is to raise the consciousness to these higher levels and to experience union, which is the inner meaning of the word "yoga."

At the mental levels, "outside" realms where unity is dominant and self-evident, some degree of unity can easily be perceived within the prevailing diversity. In common parlance, we sometimes refer to a universal "mind of nature"; also Jung postulated a collective unconscious. The best overall descriptive term is "the One Mind," signifying a unified mental field embracing and including all individual minds.

For many people this is a startling proposition when it is so definitely spelled out, instead of being left as a vague and somewhat quixotic notion. We are so proud of our own minds, of "making up our minds" after due deliberation, that we tend to resent any suggestion of sharing. This is part of the great illusion we create for ourselves. In some fashion that is hard to appreciate intellectually, *both* situations are true. We do indeed have individual minds; nevertheless they remain within the one universal mind. It is as if we appropriated to ourselves a portion of the mind ocean and fenced it off for our own use. But the fence is leaky! It is just not possible to keep our thoughts completely private nor to prevent the uninvited intrusion of other people's thoughts.

If we think about it seriously, we must realize that all this is indeed true, that indeed we half-know it already, though we are unwilling to accept it fully. Already we speak of "public opinion" and of a "climate of opinion." We commonly "open our minds" deliberately to commune with other minds in conversation and debate, and in learning situations. Of course, we know perfectly well how this is accomplished, with written or spoken words. But can we be so sure that this is the *only* means? What about telepathic communion? I suggest that telepathy is far more common than is generally believed, especially between marriage partners, family members, and close friends. A committee or study group that meets regularly can often reach a state of "being of one mind," of reaching a consensus of opinion without dissent. Moreover, in a very closely knit group there can occur a joint raising of consciousness and joint intuitive inspiration, recognized by all or most members of the group. When this happens, it is a memorable experience; what is achieved is something more than the sum of individual contributions to the discussion. There is a communion of uplifted minds, something beyond normal communication by conversation.

If the One Mind concept is acceptable, then it must follow that we also share one memory. Again, we do not normally have access to the whole of it; we appropriate to ourselves a portion of the racial memory bank, but again it is insecurely partitioned off from the whole. For ready recall we encode part of our personal memory in our brains, as explained in Chapter 9.

Before enlarging on these themes, we should complete our survey of the diagram. Proceeding outwards again to the feeling-emotional level, we seem more ready to accept the idea of empathy and shared feelings. When we are in love, we have no doubt about it at all! In religious services, particularly perhaps in the more ritualistic ones, communal feelings of devotion are very much in evidence. At a lower level it is impossible to deny the reality of mob emotions. It may be patriotism or altruism that is jointly felt so strongly, but all too often it is anger and hate that are aroused in crowds of people addressed by a demagogue. Thus in all these situations it is easy to believe in a universal sea of emotion uniting humanity, or at least large groups of people. As noted in the previous chapter, thought and emotion are almost inextricably combined. So if anyone is prepared to accept the universality of either of these, then he cannot deny it to the other.

At the physical level, where diversity is so clearly apparent, underlying unity may still be discerned. As human beings, we are obliged to accept scientific evidence that the whole of humanity is one single species; differences in skin color and facial contours between different races are no more than local variations, analogous to differences in wing coloration of the wings of moths or among Darwin's finches on the Galapagos Islands. However, many people and nations put this knowledge out of their minds and display strong antipathy towards those of other races or nationalities, even to the extent of fighting and war. Those who take the knowledge seriously enshrine it in such slogans as "the brotherhood of man," and they support organizations like the old League of Nations and now the United Nations that work for world peace, universal human rights, and fairer distribution of global resources.

Unity at the biological level extends far beyond the human race. Discovery of the genetic code expressed in DNA, and of its occurrence among all species of plants and animals, gives substance to another slogan, "the One Life." The entire biological world is united by evolutionary origins and by sharing this single "language" of the genetic code that orders the synthesis of specific proteins in all species.

Even this is not the limit of physical unity, which extends right down to inorganic matter, atoms, and subatomic particles. It has been known for a long time that chemical elements show similarities and can be arranged into "family groups" in the Periodic Table. In this century we have also learned that all the elements are made up exclusively of neutrons, protons, and electrons, their numbers increasing in regular order through the Periodic Table and their arrangement within the atom becoming more complex with increasing atomic number. Thus all atoms are members of one closely knit system. More recently still, quantum mechanics has been shown to require even closer links between subatomic particles. One theory postulates, for example, that when two particles interact, they remain indissolubly linked in some mysterious fashion, even when they become widely separated. If one of them undergoes some change, then the other instantaneously follows suit. In this context "instantaneously" means faster than any "message" could have passed from the first particle to the second, even at the speed of light, the highest velocity recognized in physics. This seemingly paradoxical postulate has been proved by Allain Aspect, in an experiment now famous among physicists. Thus we can speak of an ultimate unity that includes One Mind, One Memory, a shared emotional level, one humanity, One Life, and now one physical world.

Thus in the material world, unity is hidden but still implicit, as David Bohm explains in his book *Wholeness and the Implicate Order* (Bohm 1985). He hints, moreover, that this underlying unity is expressed in quantum theory in mathematical language. The related idea of the quantum mechanics of consciousness has been developed in considerable detail by Robert Jahn and Brenda Dunne (1986) of the Princeton University Anomalies Research unit. In a long review of their own work they allot consciousness analogies to all the physical quantities and properties involved in the various equations of quantum theory, and they expound the activities and interactions of consciousness units in these terms in an insightful manner. This treatment is applied convincingly to normal fields of consciousness and also to anomalous and otherwise inexplicable events, particularly psychokinesis and remote viewing.

TELEPATHY AND EXTRASENSORY PERCEPTION

We know all these truisms dimly, as latent thoughts, so to speak, lying dormant somewhere "at the back of the mind," but seldom brought forward for deliberate appraisal and incorporation into our normal attitude to the complexities of being. Against this background it is easier to understand such phenomena as telepathy, extrasensory perception, and intuition. If all our thinking takes place within one universal ocean of Mind, then the problem is not so much to understand how telepathy works, but why it is not commonplace. So perhaps there is no need to seek any mechanism that enables people to communicate directly.

It has been speculated that telepathy might involve electromagnetic radiation at some wavelength beyond the wide spectrum already mapped out, literally brain waves. But distance does not seem to impede telepathy; the inverse square law for the propagation of electromagnetic radiation does not apply. Alternatively, we might create "thought forms" in some mental medium and send them deliberately or unconsciously to the recipient. But if individual minds are already united within a universal Mind, then links already exist and no special mechanism need be envisaged. It should be necessary only to lower the barriers we erect in the vain attempt to keep our thoughts private. These could be lowered by love and empathy and by understanding the true nature of the situation. In practice it is not so simple. In the course of evolution we have put a lot of effort into creating and maintaining these barriers, so that they are quite strong. For telepathy, not one but two of them must be lowered or penetrated: those of the sender and those of the recipient of the thought.

When telepathy does occur, it is not easy to recognize. The thought arises quietly in the mind as though it were one's own. For example, it frequently happens that my wife makes some remark "out of the blue," unrelated to our recent conversation. I reply "Oh, I was just thinking about that." Or the roles may be reversed. So did we each happen independently and coincidentally to formulate the same thought, or did it originate with one of us and pass telepathically to the other, as we believe? And if so, who was the originator? We have not found any way to discriminate conclusively; the intruding thought arrives unannounced and masquerades to both of us as our own.

Similarly, when we receive other extrasensory information, it may be supposed that this arises directly in the recipient's mind. If the message comes through as an idea, whether or not it is expressed in words, the mind is the obvious entry gate to consciousness. But sometimes the message appears as an image resembling a scene perceived visually; this is called "clairvoyance," and some sensitives believe that the physical eyes are used, as when they gaze into a crystal ball or study the arrangement of tea leaves in a cup. Nevertheless, it seems logical to maintain that the information does come directly into the mind, and is only *referred* to the eyes, *as if* it came by normal vision. Some sensitives can "see" just as well with closed eyes, which supports this hypothesis. Moreover, as noted in Chapter 4, all ordinary visual images are reproduced on the cerebral cortex and are ultimately perceived by the mind. It is reasonable to suppose that extrasensory images are likewise presented to the mind.

In other instances the sensitive may "hear" supernatural sounds, bells, music, or spoken words, for example. Though called "clairaudience," we may again suppose that the mind receives the message directly and mistakenly refers it to the ears.

Incidentally, it may be noted that extrasensory information thus avoids the distortion and tentative interpretation that is imposed by the sense organs themselves upon normal sense perceptions. By definition, telepathy is the receipt of information from another individual. What then is the source of other types of ESP? The answer is not far to seek. It may safely be assumed, I suggest, that sensitives and mediums have an ability to "tune in" to the universal memory, which includes the collective unconscious. Besides having access to parts of their personal unconscious mind, such people can tap into the general "mind of nature." We must further assume that this mind contains not only the total memories of humanity past and present, but also some archetypal knowledge including a tentative account of *future* events; this assumption is necessary to account for instances of true prevision of events that had not yet happened at the time, but were present in the Eternal Now.

The seers themselves do not necessarily believe in this hypothesis; mediums believe they have direct communication with individuals who have died fairly recently—a sort of posthumous telepathy. Some trained seers believe that they have objective experience at higher levels of consciousness and that they can "travel" in both time and space, even visiting other planets in superphysical bodies. They may be right, but the simpler explanation seems to suffice in most instances. Moreover, the testimony of the seers themselves may not be trustworthy. If they are tapping into the universal unconscious, then this is an unreliable route to information. Certainly this applies to the personal unconscious mind, which appears to be quite amoral and also highly inventive; it does not seem to distinguish reliably between fact and fancy and uses imagery and analogy to convey its messages. It is not the source that is at fault, but the recall mechanism. Trained seers claim to have this under control, but we may wonder if this is always so. Illusion is hard to overcome at these psychic levels.

THE UNCONSCIOUS MIND

Unavoidably, the unconscious mind has been mentioned several times in this and earlier chapters. It is now time to see if we can make some sense of conflicting reports on its nature.

Unconscious thinking proceeds after its own peculiar fashion, which is not rational, nor yet just instinctive, but is certainly imaginative. As noted previously, the contents of the unconscious mind are not accessible to recall at will; items may appear spontaneously in dreams, or may pop into the conscious mind with the impact of intuitions. Such thinking may be helpful on occasions, but it is not reliable. For example, it has been shown that some supposed memories dredged up from the unconscious by hypnotic regression are purely fictitious, or they may be taken from some book, once read but totally lost to normal memory; yet they are presented to the hypnotist as personal history. The only route to deliberate recall of a specific item is to slip into the mentally relaxed state of reverie (often associated with the theta brain rhythm) and to "listen" hopefully.

One fundamental difficulty in trying to come to terms with the nature of the unconscious mind is the problem of definition. It is in fact virtually impossible to define "unconscious mind" because it is an omnibus term. It includes material from the cellar to the penthouse of the edifice of mind. The cellar contains what used to be called the "subconscious mind," that receptacle for all the thoughts we do not want to own up to, painful and disgraceful memories we prefer to forget, and so forth—the skeletons in our closet (which incidentally must be faced some day if we want to become integrated beings). At the other extreme, the penthouse corresponds with what has sometimes been called the "superconscious mind," the higher mental level, tinged with the buddhic principle, whence come the higher intuitions. Thus from what psychologists regard as a single system, the unconscious mind, there may emerge anything from the most sublime of intimations to the most bestial of erotic fantasies. Just like the conscious mind, the unconscious mind ranges over several levels; these include the higher mind (which reaches up to a level beyond the mental), pure mind, and lower mind, entwined with the desire nature; the system cannot be explained properly unless it is thus subdivided.

Just as the conscious mind represents an insecurely appropriated segment of the universal mind, the mind of nature, so the personal unconscious mind merges into the "universal unconscious." It might seem that there would be no need to discriminate between the universal mind of nature and the universal or collective unconscious. We do not have immediate access to either, but to both we have limited access via higher and lower intuitions, hunches, flashes of forgotten memories, and dreams. So in this sense there is no distinction to be drawn, but a division must still be made in respect to levels. The mind of nature is a true impersonal record of world events; if it has to be located precisely, we might suggest the level or bridge of pure mind between upper and lower mental levels. The collective unconscious, on the other hand, must be allocated to the lower mental-emotional level. It contains the personal records of humanity past and present, but it also includes our imaginings, fantasies, fears, illusions—thoughts and emotions we imagine to be private but which in reality we share, many of which we imbibe unknowingly from this shared reservoir. The collective unconscious can probably be identified with that hazy reflection of the mind of nature that has been called the "astral light." I suggest that the terms "superconscious" and "subconscious" should be used for the highest and lowest aspects; the term "unconscious" should be limited to what lies in between these, instead of being applied to the whole gamut of our unconscious thinking.

Some psychologists require the additional subdivision

of "preconscious," by which, for example, infants are equipped to learn any language they hear spoken. This preconscious level also comes into play in such activities as simultaneous translation of speeches. The translator has no time to think out his choice of words; he must perforce let them come out automatically via this preconscious thinking faculty. But if questioned subsequently, he could produce logical reasons for his choice of a particular word. Thus the mind has free access to this preconscious level, though not to the unconscious.

SPAN OF CONSCIOUSNESS

At this stage, the concept of a *span of consciousness* may usefully be introduced. It may be likened to the span of the pianist's hands on the keys, which may encompass an octave. Moving his fingers only, he can play any note within the octave, but if he wants to play higher or lower ones, he must move arm and hand along the keyboard to encompass a different span of keys. Similarly, consciousness can stretch over a limited span of levels but no further. If it wants to extend higher (or within), then it must let go of lower levels. To be more specific, the waking consciousness of an adult normally includes body and brain, feelings and emotions, and lower mind. An educated or spiritual person may have access to abstract or nonverbal ideas at the higher mental level, but as noted in Chapter 10, he then loosens his grip on brain and body. He is "living in his mind"; the span is fully extended. If then his consciousness lifts further to contact the buddhic realm, he will have lost conscious contact completely, I suggest, with body and brain and also with lower emotions. This may be only momentary, and he may remain unaware of this release unless he reflects upon it. This is a separative experience (see Chapter 12). At the other extreme, an "earthy" individual may spend much of his life within a restricted span, wallowing in feelings and emotions, hardly bothering to think for himself. The infant is also confined to this situation, through immaturity. We rarely operate at a single specific level; nearly always we are conscious over two or more adjacent levels. The span may be contracted, or it may be expanded to its limit, but not beyond; lower levels must be relinquished to attain those normally beyond our reach.

All such exalted and intuitive experiences, hard-won though they may be, fall short of the true mystical state, according to the rather stringent criteria of this book (Chapter 16). For many people, the path seems too long and arduous; they seek shortcuts to altered states of consciousness. It is well recognized that euphoric and ecstatic states can indeed be induced by chemical means, or even by mechanical or electrical stimulation of specific areas of the brain. Mild stimulants such as tea or coffee serve not only to quench the thirst, but to induce mild euphoria, and they may assist mental concentration. Alcoholic drinks are the commonest legal route to euphoria and camaraderie. A second and a third drink enhance the sensations, but at some stage of continued drinking, varying with individuals, deterioration of mental and physical stability sets in, with other familiar and embarrassing symptoms of drunkenness. Numerous plant products and synthetic drugs are used, most of them illegally (except for tobacco), to induce heightened or psychic awareness, or else dreamy somnolence.

It is very well known that almost all these substances are addictive, so that it is difficult to use them in moderation. When they are taken regularly the body's metabolism changes and actually becomes dependent on the drug. Then withdrawal symptoms become intolerable and higher doses compulsive, more to avoid these symptoms than to produce a "high." The side effects of large intakes are very unpleasant and can be fatal. It has been claimed, moreover, that the "kicks," "highs," "peak experiences" induced by drugs are inferior to those that can eventually be attained by meditative practices. In other words, the shortcuts are unsatisfactory in the long run. Some drug addicts who have been weaned from the habit have indeed turned to meditation as a more wholesome alternative. As workers in this field have remarked, the reverse change is not observed; meditators do not take to drugs. We shall return to this topic in Chapter 16 in relation to claims that have been made for valuable effects of psychedelic drugs.

RÉSUMÉ

The total field of consciousness can be subdivided into a number of distinct levels, each with unique characteristics. These are represented in alternative tabular and circular diagrams. The higher (or inner) levels are sometimes regarded as dimensions beyond the normal three of physical space. It is more satisfactory to postulate that in ascending to higher levels we do not gain extra dimensions but lose, or gain the freedom of, these three dimensions one by one. Thus at the buddhic level we gain the freedom of all three in a dimensionless, timeless realm. Individuality is triple; the highest or innermost part, virtually unrecognized in normal life, is the divine nature. The spiritual nature or transpersonal self should be in charge. Its function is often usurped by the lower or working self, centered on the body. The circular diagram also illustrates an overall unity embracing humanity, mind, memory, emotions, life, and the physical world. This concept helps to explain telepathy and other extrasensory perceptions. The nature of the unconscious mind is discussed. This omnibus term includes both superconscious and subconscious. The concept of a limited span of consciousness is introduced. The highest levels can be contacted only by letting go of the lowest. Drugs can induce euphoria and other altered states of consciousness. This shortcut is not desirable on account of side effects; nor are the experiences so gained as satisfying as those arising from long-continued meditative practices.

12

Dreaming and Other Separative States

Two mechanisms may cause us to sleep; a need for cerebral restitution and a sleep drive (which is independent of the need for restoration) to keep us occupied during darkness. The former mechanism (obligatory sleep) seems to decline steadily over the first few hours of sleep, leaving the latter hours to continue on as increasingly "optional sleep." While deep sleep appears predominantly to be obligatory, only about half of our dreaming sleep really seems to be necessary. Why we dream is another question altogether.

Jim Horne

In the previous chapter we discussed states in which consciousness is almost wholly withdrawn to higher levels, leaving body and brain relaxed and quiescent. In these meditative states, however, the body is still awake, and reversion to a more normal state in which the personality is mainly in charge can occur almost instantly. In this chapter other states are considered in which the body is not conscious; it may be asleep or in a trance, spontaneous or induced by hypnosis or other means; or again it may be in a coma, due to severe illness or injury, or it may be anesthetized or otherwise drugged. On awakening or recovery, however, the subject is sometimes aware that he had been conscious in some nonphysical body or condition, either dreaming passively or being more actively aware in an out-of-body or near-death experience.

Much has been written about sleep and dreaming, but the situation remains confused because distinctions have rarely been made between different types of sleep and dreams and their diverse functions. Various hypotheses have been proposed, supported only by conjecture or by indirect experiments susceptible to other interpretations. Arguments have followed concerning their relative merits. It has seldom been appreciated that there is room for several different hypotheses applying to the various phases of the overall sleeping and dreaming experience. It is not necessary to select a single "right" hypothesis and totally reject all others.

When we are tired, we sit or lie down to rest and recuperate. When we are very tired, we drop off to sleep. Since most of us get into this state by late evening, we make a habit of going to bed, and usually we awake refreshed next morning. So the commonsense conclusion is that the body and brain require this period of relative quiescence to recover from daily toil and pleasurable recreative exertions, and thus gain fresh energy for the morrow. To be more specific, it is supposed that cells and tissues suffer wear and tear and may get damaged or depleted by exercise, and so may use this period of sleep to get back to normal. This notion is surprisingly difficult to test. For example, the physiology of muscle fatigue is understood, and we know that rest while we are awake can effect restoration; but is there a more subtle physical restoration that demands sleep at regular intervals? Possibly not, for deprivation of sleep for several nights seems to do little or no permanent damage, though it may kill animals. Most of us probably take more sleep than we really need; perhaps the need for sleep is more psychological than physical. Certainly, prolonged deprivation does cause psychological deterioration and stress, to the point of near madness after eight nights or so. Breakdown and synthesis of protein proceed during both waking and sleeping, but the rate of synthesis is lower in sleep, due not specifically to sleep but to the fact that we commonly fast during sleep, and fasting while awake also slows protein synthesis. Anyhow, this hypothesis of bodily recuperation during sleep was more or less thrown overboard when we became aware of the physiological correlates of dreaming, and its probable psychological value. Then it was supposed that we sleep merely in order to dream at intervals. Yet the old ideas may still be right; they may still form part of the whole complex story. We may well derive both physical and psychological benefit from the long periods of deep dreamless sleep that occupy a major part of our nightly rest, as well as from the dream periods.

The brain never sleeps, any more than the heart does. Metabolism and electrical activity continue at all times in the brain, though the frequency and amplitude of the rhythms alter. So any running repairs that are needed must quite literally be done while the organ is still running. What the brain likes is change, excitement, and interesting occupation. The brain does tire, after concentrated and demanding activity like doing arithmetic or reading "heavy" books, or learning by rote. Also the brain tires when it is bored by some trivial repetitive task. When the brain tires long before bedtime, then a change of occupation may serve to revive it. One may change from study to light reading, watching television, or listening to music. Even change to an alternative demanding occupation may suffice, such as studying a different study book or solving a crossword or jigsaw puzzle.

Sleep is by no means a uniform state of blank unconsciousness. Three types of sleep have been identified: 1) deep sleep, 2) dreaming, and 3) light sleep. When we fall asleep, we generally start with a period of very deep sleep lasting about ninety minutes. A night's sleep may include three or four such episodes, of diminishing depth, followed by light sleep in the last period before waking. More interesting are the shorter interspersed episodes of dreaming sleep.

Each type of sleep shows characteristic brain rhythms (Chapter 8). In deep sleep the EEG records "spindles" of low frequency but high amplitude. In light sleep the amplitude is low but the frequency higher. Dreaming sleep is sometimes called paradoxical sleep because the brain becomes as active as it is during the waking state, whereas the body is in a sense more completely asleep than in any other stage of sleep. Muscle tone is greatly reduced and the body is nearly paralyzed; this situation can be recorded by an electromyogram (EMG). Yet some parts of the body are unusually active; there are intervals of rapid eye movement (hence the acronym REM sleep) beneath closed eyelids, as if the eyes were scanning dramatic events in the dream. These eye movements may be recorded by an electro-oculogram (EOG). In some species of animals the brain rhythms during REM sleep resemble those of the alert waking state (Chapter 8), but in man this is not so; the EEG pattern more closely resembles that of light sleep. In males the penis may be erect during all or part of the episode, even when the dream is not of an erotic nature.

Dreaming and its Significance

If subjects are awakened at any time during such episodes, they almost always report that they were dreaming. So dreams are now believed to last for around fifteen to forty-five minutes, the usual length of the REM episodes. It used to be said that dreams are compressed into the moment of waking; a person awakened by a brief noise may come to with the recollection of an elaborate dream that ended with the firing of a gun or some other noisy event providing a rational (but usually untrue) explanation for the sound. Probably dreams of *both* types occur; there is no more compulsion now to assume that all dreams are long than there was formerly to suppose that they must all be short.

If wakened during deep sleep, subjects do not report vivid dreaming. However, they do sometimes say that they were thinking coherently, or having "a different kind of dream." These observations have been pushed aside, and have not been integrated into an overall view of sleeping and dreaming. Instead, attention has been focused in recent decades on the Evans-Newman theory (Evans 1984), which holds that the brain needs these recurring dream episodes in order to update its memory store. This theory was not based on experimental evidence, and its subsequent "proof" by Dewar and Greenberg (Dewar and Greenberg 1969) does not really hold water. Indeed there seems to be more circumstantial evidence against the theory than can be adduced in its support.

Most of the arguments, for and against, are based on faulty analogies between brains and electronic computers. The two do indeed have some similarities, but in other respects they are quite different. Most electronic computers are "updated" by their operators in the normal course of usage, i.e., in working time, not while off-line. A few game-playing computers are programmed to learn by their mistakes, but again the appropriate changes in the memory bank are accomplished in the course of normal activity. The brain, however, does have regular need to update its memories; it has to convert short-term memories into intermediate-term and then into long-term memories (if the two steps can be validly distinguished). But there is ample evidence that this is done mainly by day, in the hour or so after the initial memories are acquired. The brain is adept at parallel processing; that is to say it can operate on many lines at once, processing sense impressions, making decisions, taking action via numerous commands to muscles, etc. In this respect it is far superior to any computer; so it has no difficulty in arranging the laying down of more permanent memory traces while it is busily working at daytime tasks. But even if it did need to complete the task at night, then surely it would be more likely to do so during the quiet periods of deep sleep than in the busy periods when it is inventing dreams.

Another speculative theory, again based on the behavior of certain advanced types of computers, is that the brain needs to rid itself of superfluous memories by destroying appropriate neuronic interconnections, and that it does so during periods of dreaming. But again there seems to be no compelling reason to associate such cleaning-up operations with dreams.

Such mechanistic analogies with computers cannot be expected to lead to any comprehensive theory of dreaming. It is necessary to take account of the other partners in the total adventure, namely the mind, emotions, and unconscious, the personality or lower self, and the individuality or spiritual nature. It may be noted for example that the mechanistic hypotheses take no account of the *content* of dreams. From ancient times it has been supposed that dreams have some meaning and sometimes are intended to convey symbolically some cryptic message to the dreamer. Meanings might be elucidated by reference to lists of symbols and their interpretation, though it was sometimes realized that individuals might use their own unique symbology, at least partially.

In the present century this approach was taken very

seriously by Freud and Jung and their followers, and was supposedly lifted out of its former fortune-telling character and given some sort of scientific standing. The unconscious mind, in particular its subconscious level, was held to be the main source of dream material; indeed the irrational, irresponsible, fanciful, and nonsequential character of most dreams was believed to provide clues to the nature of the subconscious. It is too well known to be worth detailing that Freud ascribed most dream content to unconscious expression of the sex drive. Jung and others played this down and identified additional drives.

In any event, an important feature of dream thinking is that the censor is taking time off. It is the censor that bans the unspeakable and deflects unwelcome thoughts into the subconscious. When it is not on duty, the brain can revel in this repressed material or may unwittingly bring up something unpleasant. It is worth recalling that during sleep the brain has access not only to its own memory stores but to the more extensive ones in the unconscious mind (as postulated in Chapter 9). Moreover, dreams are not so very different from the daydreams and fantasies that we have in relaxed wakefulness (providing limited access to the unconscious), except that the latter tend to be somewhat more rational and sequential, though still improbable. On the other hand, during sleep access to higher levels is also available if we are in the appropriate mood. This material may be brought through from what has been called the "superconscious" mind.

It seems certain, however, that much dreaming represents no more than the mulling over of recent memories and concerns, just as we worry over our problems in waking consciousness. This sort of dreaming is of no account and is best forgotten, as indeed most of it is. In contrast to the overseriousness of some psychologists, Jim Horne, director of the sleep research laboratory at Loughborough University in England, extends this notion refreshingly to the suggestion that dreams represent simply our way of keeping ourselves amused during sleep, just as we do while awake by television, recorded music, or light reading (see "The Cinema of the Mind," Horne 1982). This hypothesis, or any other concerning the purpose of dreaming, has to be judged against the near certainty that most dreams are not presented to the waking consciousness. We are aware only of dreams that happen to wake us—and most of those are promptly forgotten. Thus if dreaming is for our entertainment, the principal viewer of the dramas is the unconscious mind. This seems plausible in the light of other evidence for secret mental activity.

Scant attention has been given to the possible activities of the self and the conscious mind during sleep. Surely total unconsciousness is unthinkable. Could it not be that the more responsible elements of our total makeup are only too glad to be free from the fretful brain for a period of quiet reflection while the body sleeps? Or does the soul have nocturnal pursuits of its own, largely unknown to the waking consciousness? Such notions have indeed been seriously propounded, and we seem to get some hints of their truth in less common but more coherent dreams of "astral travel," of meeting living or dead friends and relatives, for example, during sleep.

Also relevant in this connection is the practice of sleeping on our problems. It is well known that a solution often emerges on waking, as if we had been able to devote a period of uninhibited reflection to them, aided by intuition. When we appeal to the intuition for guidance during waking consciousness, the brain is briefly transcended; in sleep it is cut off more completely, and for a longer interval, from the higher mind, thus providing an excellent opportunity for problem solving. The only difficulty is to impress the conclusions onto the brain so that they will be recalled on waking. It seems likely that a lot of serious thinking that is not revealed to the waking consciousness may take place in the watches of the night. There is some evidence for this from subjects wakened during deep sleep, who reported that they had been thinking constructively. These thoughts might well have been lost if the sleeper had been allowed to sleep on; but presumably they would have remained in the unconscious memory and might have emerged on some future occasion.

The notion of an "alter ego" quietly brooding over us while we sleep can explain another kind of dream in which a cryptic message, warning, or advice seems to be conveyed to the personality in some symbolic or allegorical fashion. This indirect approach may be used because the superconscious has no words, or because a mysterious visual image is more likely to be recalled on waking, or maybe because a direct warning would have been rejected as unwelcome.

Some people never remember their dreams; probably those we do recall are the ones that woke us up. These too are soon forgotten unless they are particularly vivid and compelling. So should we pay more attention to our dreams? It is possible to cultivate a receptive attitude if we believe it to be worthwhile. The technique is to remain relaxed yet attentive on waking, making a gentle effort to remember the dream without snatching at it, so to speak. One must stalk the happening, as one might stalk a wild creature to obtain a photograph, taking great care not to scare it away. Preferably, impressions should be recorded immediately either by jotting them down or, less disturbingly, by whispering them into a tape recorder kept handy by the bed. But is it worth the effort? Since most dreams are essentially meaningless, the answer would seem to be no. On the other hand, regular recording might encourage reception of more serious kinds of dreams which would be a pity to lose. Most people have something better to do; they just cannot spare the time anyhow. But after retirement from career and active life, dream watching may provide a new interest. In time it might lead to familiarity with one's secret nocturnal life.

LUCID DREAMS

Many dreams comprise episodes that we see simply as observer. In others we ourselves seem to play a role, but one that is imposed upon us, as if we were acting out a drama devised by some other playwright. Besides these wholly passive dreams, there are some in which we play a more active role. The scenery usually is still imposed, but we choose what we do in it. These are the so-called "lucid dreams," in which we are aware at the time that we *are* dreaming, and we deliberately take some control over the course of events.

Keith Hearne (Hearne 1981) has described some interesting dream laboratory work on lucid dreams. His main difficulty was that nothing in the EEG or other recordings indicates when the subject is having a *lucid* dream. Because the body is nearly paralyzed during dream episodes, the subject cannot signal to the experimenter, by pressing a switch for example. However, two bodily functions escape this paralysis—the eyes and the breathing; either can be used for signalling by prearranged codes. Thus deliberate left-to-right eye movements can be used to signal the onset of a lucid dream, and also the onset or end of flying episodes. The end of the lucid dream is usually marked by the subject waking up and being able to describe the dream. In these experiments, lucid dreams lasted for one to six minutes, and usually occurred between 6:30 and 8:00 a.m. Strong emotions correlated with increased heart rate, but emotional conflict caused immediate awakening. One subject could control lucid dreaming by acting upon instructions given a few hours previously.

Even more interesting were experiments on the deliberate induction of lucid dreams. When the REM state was shown by the EOG recording, subjects were given a slight electric shock at the wrist as a prearranged signal to "wake" into lucidity within the dream in progress. This strategem worked with eight out of ten subjects, each tested on one night only.

A variant on this situation is "night nurse paralysis." The stimulus then is a patient calling or ringing a bell for attention. The nurse, sleeping on duty, is not fully awakened but goes into a lucid dream in which she seems to drag herself with difficulty to the patient's bedside, but is then unable to do anything effective while in the dream state. The same sort of thing can happen to people who are not nurses. My wife recalled an occasion when she was dozing in the afternoon and was alerted by steps on the path outside. In a few moments of lucid dreaming, she seemed to get up and, looking out the window, recognized the coal merchant coming to deliver some coal. She was awakened when he rang the doorbell.

Programmed Dreams

A few people have been able to take a further step and have succeeded in preprogramming their dreams. They may decide in advance to visit some place or a particular person, and sometimes on waking they recall having done in their dreams what they intended. The Mexican Indian "sorcerer" don Juan taught his pupil to do this; he called it "doing dreaming." For example, he bade his pupil Carlos Castaneda (Castaneda 1976) to try to see his own hands in a dream. Recently some groups in America, Canada, and Europe have taken up the pursuit; members plan in advance that one person will try to travel in a dream and meet another designated individual. On occasions both participants have been able to recall such a meeting. A group in Virginia reported a high degree of success in such trials, including some for which a specified meeting place was agreed on in advance. In one dramatic experiment, all ten members of the group planned to meet on a bus in a joint dream, and most of them were there.

More stringent tests were organized with two new ten-member groups, this time with people who had never met in their waking lives and who had no prior interest in dreams. Over a period of four months, seven target dates and meeting places were nominated. After these occasions, participants sent in reports of their dreams, which were circulated to the other participants. Again striking successes were noted. Strangers correctly described the appearance of other participants whom they had met only in mutual dreams. They also correctly described the designated meeting sites, previously unknown to any participant.

In similar independent experiments, meetings were successfully arranged between people living long distances apart. It was even suggested that business associates might arrange to sort out their problems in dream meetings! This is not so ridiculous as it may sound. It may well be that such meetings do occur, without prearrangement and without either participant recalling the details. They know only that the problem resolved itself during the night. Unremembered dream meetings might also explain the well-known phenomenon in scientific research that important discoveries are often made almost simultaneously in different laboratories. As noted in Chapter 11, our thoughts are not as private as we suppose; they may become known to others by unintended thought transference. Now we learn, possibly with dismay, that even dreams are not always private.

OBJECTIVE OUT-OF-BODY EXPERIENCES

So far in this book we have consideed higher states of consciousness that are experienced only *subjectively*, and indeed that is the *only* manner in which most people become aware of such states. Increasingly, however, we read of people who have had *objective* experiences of other states. They suddenly found themselves vividly conscious in a subtle nonmaterial body; in some instances they were simultaneously aware of their physical body as an external object, usually though not always asleep or unconscious. Surprisingly, this body held little interest for them because active consciousness was centered wholly or almost wholly in the separate subtle body.

It might be expected that such an event would prove extremely disconcerting or even terrifying, but this is not so. Instead, the happening is usually greeted with a sense of familiarity and joyfulness. It is as if one had stepped out of a fancy dress costume and mask, to recognize oneself truly for the first time. It is like coming awake to a dream world, and discovering that after all that is the real world; waking consciousness by contrast is a stifling existence in which one has been obliged to play a part within a heavy, clumsy physical body, subject to aches and pains and all manner of restrictions (Smith 1986). This condition has been called out-of-body experience (OBE); a variant is near-death experience (NDE), which may occur in the interval between drowning or heart failure, for example, and resuscitation. In some instances the subject will remember being in a subtle body after what he believed to be death, and having remarkable experiences. Raymond Moody (Moody 1976) has collected records of many such cases, and has described some fifteen distinct experiences that subjects recall on being brought back to life. No single subject reported all of them, but every one did report at least half of them, with convincing consistency. Some of these events are the same as those reported for OBE, but there are additional features. See also Margot Grey's recent book on NDEs of English subjects (Grey 1985).

Anyone who has never had such an experience—and that means most of us—may be puzzled as to how it differs from dreaming. That is a reasonable query, even though it may seem laughable to anyone who *has* actually experienced an out-of-body or near-death state, so different are they from either normal dreaming or waking consciousness. They can arise in at least two ways. One may seem to awaken from a lucid dream, or from unconsciousness, to find that instead of coming back to the waking state, one has instead "gone forward," so to speak, to "wake" into vivid awareness in a subtle body. In this condition the senses seem sharper, the body more sprightly and unencumbered, the mind more alert, and the soul joyous and free. Most of those who enter this state report it as startlingly, wonderfully, and unmistakably different from familiar conditions. The second way in which this condition may arise is directly from the waking state, presumably with a momentary and unnoticed break in consciousness. Then it is as if one fell asleep, yet remained awake, but in this new, different state. Whichever way it occurs, its reality is sometimes confirmed for the subject by a glimpse of the inert physical body.

Many more of us may in fact have such experiences during sleeping hours, without ever being aware of them in normal consciousness, as indicated earlier in this chapter. Occasionally one may wake with the vivid memory of such an event. But unless one knows of the possibility of awareness in a subtle body, the event comes through simply as an exceptionally vivid dream. The brain presents it in this guise, and may even weave the event into the fabric of an ordinary dream. At other times one may wake with no precise memory but with an insistent sense of participation in strange and wondrous happenings.

All such experiences in which consciousness is wholly in a subtle body, or split between this and the physical body, are called "separation" by J. M. H. Whiteman (1961) who has made a penetrating analysis of these and more exalted states. He distinguishes three types: 1) primary, in which the physical body is unconscious, e.g. asleep or entranced; 2) secondary, in which consciousness is divided between physical and subtle bodies; and 3) tertiary, in which consciousness is neither in nor out of the body (or is in and out simultaneously), as in many mystical experiences in which awareness of the body is blotted out, yet one's senses and faculties seem to be actually enhanced (increased intelligence and love, for example). In a later book (Whiteman 1986) five types of separation are distinguished. A feature common to them all is mind-brain dissociation. In secondary separation, for example, the diminished consciousness in the physical body is looked after by the brain alone, which is quite capable of carrying on routine activities and indulging in small talk.

SUBTLE BODIES

Curious uncertainty persists as to the number and nature of the subtle bodies we use. The early theosophical books were quite explicit; there was a body for each "plane," and each was composed of the "subtle matter" of the corresponding level. Later writers have come to think that this exposition was in effect forced upon Annie Besant and C. W. Leadbeater, who wrote many books on the subject, by the materialistic, mechanistic character of nineteenth century science. They had to conform with its terminology to some degree, so they postulated bodies composed of successively higher grades of matter, each more tenuous than the last. There was no other language in which their experiences at higher levels of consciousness could be expressed, so as to be understood by general readers. Such physicalistic ideas may have outlived their usefulness, though in a more subtle interpretation they accord with the Indian Sankhya philosophy and with some later theosophical writings.

The scheme of overlapping levels of consciousness presented in this book, corresponding to the composite character of human nature, is hardly compatible with this notion of a multiplicity of permanent bodies. I offer as an alternative the concept of just two composite, permanent subtle bodies. The first would correspond with our normal working self or personal nature, embracing lower mental and emotional levels. In waking consciousness this would be coupled to the physical body, including its etheric component. At death, this and the gross physical body are lost. The second composite subtle body would correspond with our spiritual nature, embracing higher mental, buddhic, and atmic levels. However, this second alternative also has unsatisfactory features. When we are in separation, we should usually be in the lower of these subtle bodies, that of the personal nature. But this view implies that if we then ascend to higher levels, we should be obliged to slip out of this body into our spiritual one—a kind of second separation. I cannot recall any mention of such an event in the extensive literature. It would also be necessary to suppose that both bodies are protean in character and able to change their form in different circumstances.

Whiteman has proposed a third alternative (private communication). He affirms that in some fifty years of separative experience he has appeared in thousands of bodies. From personal experience and citing the authority of Gautama Buddha, he holds emphatically that we have *no permanent subtle bodies* at all. At each occasion we create a fresh one appropriate to conditions at that time. He insists also that even at the highest levels we do manifest in some human-like form, but one that is far more beautiful and perfect than the physical body. This is the concept that is most fully in line with current thinking in physics and philosophy; but it may not yet be generally acceptable.

It may well be that this third alternative most closely corresponds to conditions of separation during life, while after death the second alternative applies. Lacking the physical body, there would be greater need for permanent subtle bodies. Moreover, there *are* accounts in both spiritualistic and theosophical literature of a "second death" at which consciousness passes from one subtle body to another more spiritual one. It seems likely that the idea of a span of consciousness (Chapter 11) can be extended to conditions after death. While centered at a particular level, consciousness may extend to levels above and below.

Unfortunately, there are no words to convey precisely the nature of objective separative experience. Whatever is said is bound to be misunderstood to some degree. Even when we have such experiences ourselves, the early ones are liable to be undeveloped or to contain elements of fantasy, and will therefore be atypical. We need to gain familiarity with our (temporary?) subtle bodies, and it may take years of practice before we discover and make full use of all their capabilities.

The most frequently reported separations are out-of-body experiences and near-death experiences in primary separation. I have reviewed reports of such experiences in another recent book (Smith 1986). Instead of elaborating further here, I shall consider the nature of the duplicate world in which most of these subjects find themselves.

THE DUPLICATE WORLD

Most people who have out-of-body experiences find themselves in a condition that closely resembles the familiar physical world, though they are withdrawn from it in the sense that they can no longer interact with this world as in normal waking consciousness. They cannot move things, for example—the hand just passes through the object; walls are no barrier—it is possible to pass right through them without hindrance. The obvious explanation is that in this state subjects still see the ordinary physical world, and indeed that is what most of them believe, even some experienced sensitives. The more perceptive among them, however, have discovered that although this world *resembles* the physical one, it is *not identical* with it. For example, one viewer found, when he checked later, that the paving stones in the road that he had noticed while out of body were arranged in quite a different pattern from the real one. Another, who got no further than his bedroom in the OBE, observed a bundle of dirty linen in a corner of the room. On returning to the body, he saw that in fact there was no such bundle; but it had been there the previous day. Other instances of such a time-shift can be cited. For example, some subjects find themselves in a house they had occupied years previously. Moreover, lighting conditions differ from those of the physical world; often there appears to be a general diffused glow without any obvious source, even at night.

Incidentally, transport in OBE states has other-worldly characteristics. From habit we may appear to walk, but flying, as if on a magic carpet, is more usual; or the desire to be in some particular place or with a specified person may be gratified almost instantly without any sense of movement at all. So there is an element of fantasy, of unreality, about this world. It is like a recollection of the physical world, with the forgotten items filled in by the creative imagination. But in the subtle body we may travel beyond familiar territory, yet still be aware of our surroundings, sometimes in surprising detail.

What then is the nature of this strange realm, which Whiteman designates "the duplicate world"? It might be suggested that it has no real existence, that it is merely a creation of our memory and imagination. But the word "our," when used in this context, has at least two different connotations. In general, the word signifies the whole of humanity—the memory and imagination that are communal; this world seems to correspond in part to Jung's collective unconscious. But locally we fill in details and imagine for ourselves what we cannot recall. This implies that the duplicate world is a fluidic construction, partly communal, partly personal, and by no means identical for every observer.

One might think that in principle this idea is something that could be checked; two or more people could leave their bodies together, remain together, and compare their experiences. The experiment may have been tried already, by Monroe's "explorer group" for example (Smith 1986). But in practice it would probably be meaningless. If two people enter this domain intending to examine the same phenomenon, then it is likely that their observations will agree because they will unconsciously tend to mold the phenomenon in unison. This protean domain is not stable like the physical world; to a large extent the observer will see what he expects to see; it will be "true" for him or her, but not necessarily the same for others.

Incidentally, we have to ask ourselves whether the physical world itself is as stable as we used to suppose. In recent decades, it too has taken on something of this protean quality. Scientists observing certain phenomena, especially at subatomic dimensions, are uncertain whether they perceive particles or waves. The same entities show different properties when studied in different ways with appropriate instruments. The behavior of other systems, especially at very high velocities or at great distances, demands relativity or quantum mechanics for explanation; in such situations commonsense Newtonian mechanics are inapplicable. We are left wondering what does remain fixed and dependable. The only true answer may be what seers and sages throughout the ages have proclaimed—all is illusion, *maya*, except the Eternal One.

Reverting to the duplicate world, we may reflect that if it did not exist already, we should need to create it, to reassure ourselves by its familiarity when we find ourselves away from the physical body. But there is still something unsatisfactory about the notion that it is wholly imaginary. In normal life, a sculptor can hold his statue or figurine in his thoughts for a while, but he needs some substance—wax, clay, plaster, wood, ivory, stone—that he can mold or chisel to give his image enduring form. Correspondingly, we surely need some subtle ideoplastic *substance* from which to create and shape this protean but abiding duplicate world.

These suggestions have a familiar ring to them; they resemble in many respects the descriptions of the astral plane, as given by theosophists and spiritualists. This is said to be the realm in which we find ourselves after death. In the out-of-body condition or the near-death experience or separation, we are only lightly linked to the physical body; it seems probable that conditions would be similar to those immediately after death, when the link is finally severed. The present reflections seem to confirm that this may well be so (see also Smith 1986). The astral plane is said to be a real world, but its scenery is said to be fashioned largely by individual and collective imagination. It too is a protean world, and there are no bounds to the forms it can assume. So there is ample scope within it for the inclusion of this duplicate world that so closely resembles the physical one. If that is the world that still interests a visitor in separation, then that is where he will be.

It is true that the lower division of the astral plane has been described by Leadbeater as a gloomy, exceedingly depressing domain frequented by suicides, drunkards, and other intensely earthbound types. But the lower astral levels can accommodate this duplicate world in addition to Leadbeater's suicides' domain. The respective inhabitants need be no more aware of each other than early Europeans were of Australian Aborigines. However, Leadbeater's picture of the astral world seems to me too restricted and also too sharply stratified; indeed it is not so much a place as a state of consciousness.

The strangeness of objective experience in the subtle body can be explained in part by the fact that in that state we are almost entirely out of touch with the brain. Many subjects have reported that in separation they can think more clearly and one-pointedly; presumably, this is due to freedom from the distractions and dreamlike fantasizing of the restless brain. Insofar as experiences in that state are colored by memory and imagination, these are necessarily intrusions from the unconscious mind, since the brain memory is inaccessible.

It is possible to attempt some reconciliation between the concepts of a pre-existing duplicate world and a realm fashioned largely by our imagination. Even in waking consciousness we commonly recognize that we regard the world differently on separate occasions according to our moods. When we feel supremely happy, we view the world through "rose-tinted spectacles," for example. Freed partially (or wholly at death) from the physical body and brain, we may well believe that imagination has a freer rein. But unless it is very strong and persistent, we need not suppose that we actually mold the tenuous substance of the duplicate world. For the most part, we carry our personal imaginings around with us, and do not impose them upon our surroundings or upon the attention of the other inhabitants, who in turn are wrapped up in their own ideas.

A puzzling feature of this kind of experience is that an individual may appear to be present in *two* distinct bodies. In separation, he is aware of the subtle body in which his consciousness is centered, but he may also see what he takes to be his physical body. Muldoon, wandering about the house at night in separation, "saw" his relatives asleep in the bed and simultaneously their subtle bodies floating above them, evidently wrapped in their own thoughts and paying no attention to their surroundings (Muldoon and Carrington 1963). We have already established that the actual physical world and its inhabitants are not visible in separation. It is confusing to suggest that people can appear to have two astral bodies. It is preferable to suggest that one body is experienced as real, while the other is illusory, a kind of imitation or replica or thought form of the physical body, presented to us when we are conscious at the astral level but still fixated upon physical life. Probably it is not an actual vision in real time; it may not correspond with the exact condition of the physical body at that moment. This is suggested by a few published accounts. The experience resembles that of the man who saw a bundle of laundry in his bedroom while in separation. It *had* been there the previous day. It is no wonder that usually we cannot interact with these illusory presentations of our associates in the ordinary world, even though we may believe we see them.

It may help in comprehending the situation to suggest that physical events are instantly impressed upon "the mind of nature," and that in our subtle bodies we "tune in" to those parts of the record that concern us.

An alternative is that in separation we might see, not dense physical bodies, but the etheric bodies or doubles of ourselves and other living people. This is doubtful for various reasons. It is quite untenable when we experience a time-shift and seem to see events of the past including people physically dead, or to see presentiments of the future. These considerations provide a clue to the nature of other seemingly physical objects seen in the duplicate world, whether inanimate or living; we must suppose that these too are astral counterparts, spuriously invested with solidity by imagination exercised quite unconsciously by the viewer. He need never discover his mistake unless he tries to touch any such object or person and meets no resistance. On the other hand, it has been reported that it *is* possible to experience touching someone while in separation, provided the other person is also in separation or dead.

It must be added that in separation we are not obliged to remain in the duplicate world. If we determine to do so, we can rise to higher levels of consciousness, and probably more easily than we can while in the physical body. After death, it has been said that we make an orderly ascent through these levels. This may be the general rule, but I suspect we flutter up and down at times, just as we do in physical life.

RÉSUMÉ

Such consciousness as we enjoy at higher levels is usually subjective. However some people have objective awareness of such states in lucid dreams, OBE, and NDE. A number of hypotheses have been proposed to explain the functions of sleep and dreaming. They need not all be mutually exclusive. We probably do need sleep, as commonly supposed, for the recuperation of the tired body and brain, and possibly also to update the brain's memory bank and to eliminate unwanted memories. It seems unlikely however that dreams facilitate these operations. Sleep of three types—deep, dreaming (REM sleep), and light—recur at intervals each night. Few dreams are recalled accurately on waking. The usual inconsequential passive dreams, in which we have access to unconscious as well as brain memories, may just be a way of keeping ourselves amused at night, a continuation of our daytime need for entertainment. But there are more meaningful dreams in which we may travel and meet people. These merge into lucid dreams in which we play an active role. It is possible to prearrange some control of dreams. In objective separation we usually find ourselves in a "duplicate world" which resembles but is not identical with the normal world of waking consciousness. The nature of this realm is discussed.

13

Holism, Monism, and Dualism

Light is what enfolds all the universe in its generalized sense, it is the means by which the entire universe unfolds into itself. It is energy, information, content, form and structure. It is the potential of everything.
David Bohm

This chapter brings together and enlarges upon ideas that have been broached in earlier chapters. The terms "holism," "wholeness," "unity," and "monism" have been used more or less synonymously. I suggest that a distinction can usefully be made. The first pair has been used particularly by philosophers and scientists, notably by Smuts and Bohm (Bohm 1985), to denote the *mental concept* of the state of unity. The second pair has been used frequently by mystics to denote *the state itself*, which can be entered into only in a state of exalted consciousness beyond all mentation. These are distinctions worth perpetuating. "Spirit" may be added to the second pair.

RESOLUTION OF DUALITIES

As noted in Chapter 1, the "strong dualism" proclaimed by Eccles is in fact not classical dualism between pairs of fundamental opposites, but a lesser dualism between intimately related components of one system, the brain-mind complex. Such a duality can be resolved intellectually; we can, if we so wish, consider this complex as a whole; or we can go further and consider the whole man as a unit. Such mental resolution leads to a situation of wholeness or holism, but not of monism, according to my definition. On the other hand, the dualism of ultimate opposites such as Spirit and matter, or good and evil, can only be fully resolved in mystical consciousness; such resolution leads to unity or monism as a state of being, not just as a way of thinking.

It seems likely that the paradoxes introduced into physics by quantum theory can similarly find completely satisfactory resolution only in mystical consciousness. A recent book, *The Ghost in the Atom* (Davies and Brown 1986), includes interviews with leading physicists, but their differing attempts at intellectual resolution of these paradoxes are to some degree mutually contradictory.

GRADATION BETWEEN UNITY AND DIVERSITY

At the opposite extreme to all these lie "diversity" and "dualism," "substance" and "matter." But the opposites are not starkly and sharply set apart. The universe is pervaded by duality, yet unity persists; a gradation may be perceived between the two. In the highest realm, Spirit is the ruling partner. Substance is tenuous in the extreme, almost without power. But it is present and it gains effectiveness in the descent through the levels. So at the other extreme, in the physical world, substance has become dense matter and Spirit almost subdued. The midpoint at which the opposites are equal partners can probably be taken as the middle of the mental realm, the segment described as pure mind in Diagram 1 in Chapter 11. This notion of gradation may be illustrated

(crudely) by the simple Diagram 3, but this must not
be taken too literally. At the mental bridge, where the
two lines of the diagram cross, Spirit and matter are
equally potent. Of these two pairs, Spirit and substance,
unity and duality, which pole then is real? Fundamen-
tally, the only possible answer is that *both* are equally
real, but this is not the answer that is usually given.

According to the Eastern tradition (Chapter 15), humanity emerged from Spirit aeons ago, and gradually
descended during long ages through the levels of consciousness towards total immersion in the physical world.
Thence we are destined to rise again, carrying with us
the essence of what we have gleaned through many lives.

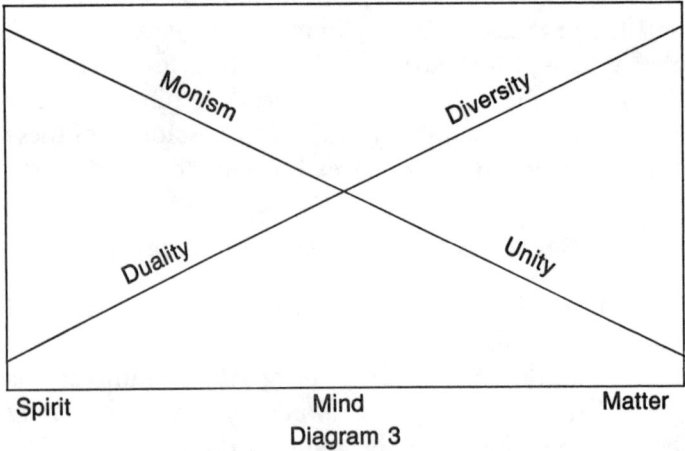

Diagram 3

Humanity is now well past the nadir, the midway
point. Its saints and seers have forged ahead as our advance guard. Further progress will be rapid (on a cosmological time scale) once humanity fully accepts
responsibility for its own cultural evolution, and ceases
to rely on the gods for guidance. So *for us* now and
henceforth, unity is the goal, and that which we seek
in our quest is what we call "reality" (Chapter 16). But
we are by no means finished with duality; our work in

the world must be conducted along dualistic lines for long aeons yet. Our logical thinking processes and their expression in language are both inescapably rooted in duality. Thus we are chained to duality; yet many creative thinkers are uncomfortable with this situation.

PSEUDO-MONISM

Scientists crave unifying principles and seek unitary hypotheses. So also do some philosophers and yogis. But some in all three groups try to take a shortcut and are satisfied that they have already found unity. They achieve their pseudo-monistic position by the simple expedient of denying or ignoring one of the aspects of duality and claiming that everything can be explained by the one that remains. Materialists reject the world of the Spirit and indeed everything nonmaterial. Conversely, some yogis turn their backs on the material world as illusory and/or worthless.

Materialistic scientists maintain that the physical world is all there is. Life emerged automatically from organic matter produced chemically on the primitive earth. Living forms evolved through the agencies of chance and natural selection. Thought and feelings arose from brain activity. Thus a satisfying but false unity is found. This position is strongly maintained as the obviously true state of affairs by highly intelligent scientists, Nobel laureates among them. This is so only because it is possible to build a highly consistent body of science without reference to any higher levels of existence, or to any intelligence beyond what is held to have arisen in man by natural evolution. This in turn is possible only because the physical world really does exhibit autonomy to a very high degree. It functions according to physical laws that have been discovered to operate, not just qualitatively but also quantitatively,

to an extremely high degree of precision. There seems
to be no need to invoke any guidance or interference
by Divine Intelligence, nor any causes initiated at higher
levels.

This position in science is sincerely held not only by
materialists but by religious people who do believe in
higher states. They must of course accept duality in the
manifested world. Also they must modify the extreme
materialist position in a very significant way by claiming that physical laws are in reality divine laws operating
in the physical world. The autonomy is real, they proclaim, but it is divinely and immutably ordained from
the beginning.

Such a position could be held with complete honesty
until around the first quarter of this century. Then the
notion of complete autonomy in the physical world
began to fray at the edges, though it is still accepted by
materialists. Uncertainties showed themselves in the
realms of the very small—in nuclear physics—and the
very large—in astronomy and cosmology, and also in
biological behavior, especially in man, and in the paranormal. Thus at subatomic dimensions our commonsense
world of sensory observation has to be stretched to embrace quantum mechanics, material particles that sometimes behave like wave-packets, and (as I believe) we
are in effect extending physics into the etheric levels.
Also we must accept that matter and energy are inter-
convertible in some circumstances. In the far reaches
of outer space, we are obliged to extend the ideas of
Euclid and Newton to include those of Einstein and his
followers. Our concepts must now include relativity,
space-time integration, and new geometries involving
curved space. In the biological realm we *do* see (unless
we blinker ourselves as the materialists do) the influence
of Divine Intelligence in evolution, and the action of

mind upon matter via the brain. In man alone, it is said, is wrought the miracle of the coordination of highest Spirit with lowest matter. Paranormal phenomena of all kinds, which cannot be explained by known physical laws, always involve human beings.

There is an alternative way to find a spurious unity. It is the way adopted by some mystics and yogis who proclaim that only Spirit is real. Matter is regarded by some schools of yogis as having no real existence; other schools concede its existence, but regard it as valueless, even as evil. Either way, Nirvana is the goal, not service in the world. Most Westerners find the physical world so insistent that they cannot entertain such beliefs, but they are sincerely held and taught in some Indian ashrams. The objective world is said to be maya, illusion.

Are such statements intended to deny the very existence of the world? Surely it is only our usual *attitude* towards the world that is false and illusory, and especially so if we suppose there is nothing beyond the physical. Most people regard their environment in dualistic fashion, as external, as not-self. But in mystical experience we come to realize that we are integral with the whole universe. Such ideas are brought out very clearly in Ken Wilber's books *The Spectrum of Consciousness* and *The Atman Project* and in Chaudhuri's *Integral Yoga* (Chaudhuri 1965).

A proper goal for Westerners is to achieve mystical consciousness, to realize unity as an actual experience. This allows the dualistic world to be seen in proper perspective. It becomes tolerable but no longer desirable. Then gradually the center of consciousness is raised till mystical consciousness becomes habitual. The delights of earthly life pale in contrast; they may still be enjoyed in passing, but they are no longer sought after. So comes gradual release from "the bondage of the three worlds," without too much suffering. The personal ego "dies" as the spiritual nature takes over, and peace is found in doing such work in the world as seems proper.

Such disciplines are being advocated by nonreligious bodies, especially in America, under the description of "transpersonal psychology." In relation to the gradation of duality here presented, it must be accepted that mystical consciousness, at least in its early stages, is release into a realm where unity is dominant, *but not absolute.* Its impact may be so great that one supposes it to be absolute, but actually these early stages are only the first steps into higher realms, as Eastern scriptures proclaim. There is even greater bliss to come.

Resumé

Holism and wholeness may be held to denote the *mental concepts* of the state of unity; monism and unity are *the state itself,* as known in mystical consciousness. Their opposites are duality, diversity, and matter. But there is a gradation between the pairs of opposites, Spirit being supreme in the highest realms but diminishing in power in descent towards the physical world, where matter holds almost undivided sway. The midpoint where both Spirit and matter are equal (Diagram 3) is middle mind. Mankind is held to have descended from Spirit through many lives, and is now embarked on the return journey. But worldly affairs must perforce still be conducted in dualistic fashion. False unitary states may be created by denying one or the other of the opposites, leading to materialism or world-negating yogas. The Western goal should be transpersonal psychology and mystical awareness of unity, leading to enlightened conduct in the world.

14

Intuition, Creativity

Scientists are usually too proud or too shy to speak about creativity and "creative imagination"; they feel it to be incompatible with their conception of themselves as "men of facts" and rigorous inductive judgement. The role of creativity has always been acknowledged by inventors, because inventors are often simple unpretentious people who do not give themselves airs, whose education has not been dignified by courses on scientific method.

Sir Peter Medawar

Analysis of the levels of consciousness in Chapter 11 makes it easier to understand the nature of intuition. It is not limited to understanding that comes from one specific level. It comprises, rather, the brief lifting of consciousness to whatever level lies immediately beyond one's normal span. For example, to the infant his first thought must be a wondrous event. For older people concrete thinking is commonplace. But from time to time they may receive hunches or minor intuitions of a pragmatic and utilitarian character. These may involve recall of some forgotten and wanted piece of information, or even something so trivial as the most appropriate word to express something we are writing or talking about.

As noted earlier, the flashes arrive with the impact of the more spiritual type of intuition, and I suggest they too are appropriately categorized as intuitions. The characteristics of the impact, from whatever source, are suddenness and unexpectedness on the one hand, and an accompanying sense of rightness on the other. It is the "Eureka experience," or when it becomes more familiar, the "aha, that's right" reaction.

These lesser intuitions clearly derive from the personal unconscious or from some more general pool of knowledge in the collective unconscious. I recall two particularly vivid personal examples. As a young research chemist in industry, I had been puzzling over a problem. It happened that I was living only a few miles from the laboratory, so I sometimes rushed home for a quick lunch via the London Inner Circle underground line. As I reached the station, I heard a train approaching, so I ran helter-skelter down the stairs, two treads at a time. Between one leap and the next the answer to my problem flashed into my mind. I caught the train!

Some years later I was developing the synthesis of a new drug. One step was liable to produce a mixture of isomers. Having crystalized out the desired one in poor yield, I was left with an oily residue. A message then came to me "out of the blue": "Try iodine." This recalled something my conscious mind had quite forgotten, namely that iodine sometimes catalyzes the interconversion of geometrical isomers of the syn-anti type. I accordingly warmed my residue with a trace of iodine, and was able to crystallize out a further crop of the required isomer, dramatically increasing the overall yield, to commercial advantage. Such lower intuitions are of pragmatic, utilitarian value. They are quite distinct from higher intuitions of philosophical or spiritual content.

Concrete thinking includes thinking *about* abstract principles formulated in concrete terms. But this is by no means the same as using the higher mind. To the youth or adult, the first experience of thinking in an abstract, wordless fashion comes as a startling adventure; it is one's first probing into a new mode of thinking, the use of the higher mind. For many people, intuition remains at this level; it is thus an expansion of consciousness from lower to higher mind. It concerns moments when concepts such as love, justice, or faith are revealed as abstract general principles in their own right, and not just as specific examples encountered in normal life.

Such mental events certainly have an intuitional character, but the word "intuition" is sometimes reserved for revelations at a somewhat higher level, when the higher mind is more positively infused with "the light of buddhi." Such intuitions are of an uplifting, spiritual nature; they are transcendent and transpersonal in character. As Emerson says in his essay "The Oversoul," "The soul answers never by words, but by the thing itself that is inquired after." An intuition of this nature is "a direct perception of truth at its core...the intuitive faculty is one which transcends reason and makes it obsolete as the final authority" (Burden 1987). Reason must, however, be brought to bear on the revelation subsequently in order to "explain" it. In the process it is perforce stepped down, gaining in clarity and utility, but losing innocence, purity, and generality.

Annie Besant has given an interesting example of the operation of lower and higher mind and intuition. It concerns concrete and abstract triangles. She claims that after long practice it is possible to create in the higher mind the abstract idea of "triangularity." It is the mental image of a kind of "hypergeometrical figure" that embraces triangles of all shapes and sizes, having all possible angles from just over 0° to nearly 180°. This image exists as an external reality only at the formless level of the higher mind. It is an intuition pertaining to that level, which recognizes the outer, contrasting with the buddhic level which recognizes the inner. The process of creating this image and "seeing" it with the mind's eye becomes intelligible only if it is practiced. Any attempt to bring the abstract idea down to the level of the lower mind causes it to cascade into a fountain of particular triangles of every possible kind.

RELIABILITY OF INTUITION

Are intuitions always right? Are they infallible? Many people imagine they are and accept them at face value. More experienced and cautious individuals, however, come to learn that intuitions are *not* uniformly reliable. So how can this arise? In the case of minor intuitions of a practical nature, it is easy to see that the unconscious mind may produce the wrong information, just as a computer does if the wrong keys are pressed. Sometimes the fault is spotted at once, by some faculty that Eccles calls the recognition memory, and the search must start again. In any event, an intuition ought to be checked, by experiment when appropriate, by consulting a reference book, or in some other way.

It is sometimes said that the higher intuitions cannot be wrong because they involve the buddhic level where falsity is impossible. This may be accepted, but nevertheless what is received may still turn out to be faulty. In these cases the explanation lies in a transmission error. The intuition arrives naked, so to say, as a pure idea or symbol, not clothed in words or even in concrete thought. In order to capture it in some intelligible and memorable shape, we have perforce to formulate it, using whatever mental equipment and vocabulary we happen to possess. The inexperienced person, not skillled at putting ideas into words, may arrive at a thoroughly misleading formulation. He is apt to twist his revelation into conformity with preconceived notions of dubious validity, thus completely garbling the fresh insight he had been granted. Even worse, he may be wrong in supposing that he has received an intuition "from above." What came through may be no more sublime than his own imagining or wishful thinking. Thus may the uncontrolled and prejudiced personality mislead itself and perpetuate wrongful thinking. Nothing can cure this state of affairs but experience and the cultivation of an open mind, willing to concede that it can sometimes be wrong.

How then can we ensure the receipt of true and valid intuitions when they are needed? The first thing to note is that the faculty of intuition can be wooed and besought, but it cannot be commanded. If the higher intuition comes at all, it is as an act of grace, in response to a selfless need. This may seem to be a fickle gift, but it is not really so. It is possible so to order one's life that inspiration flows reliably and continuously, as when writing a book, for example. This condition is not achieved by just wishing, but by hard work and intense preparation. For a start, the mind must be cleared as completely as possible of attachments to preconceived or generally accepted ideas. They need not be cast out utterly; there is no necessity for an empty and blank mind. It may well be filled with ideas that seem logical and useful. What must be done is to let go of any *attachment* to such ideas. Let them be held as a working framework or paradigm, but lightly, always recognizing that they are not final and immutable, but subject to improvement or even total replacement as fresh understanding comes. This is a progressive long-continuing undertaking; the right habit of mind builds up with practiced and determined cultivation of awareness. Intuitions do not flow into a lazy mind. Besides being well-stocked with the mental tools of one's trade, so to speak, the mind must be both active and receptive.

Thus two paths may be postulated for the flow of intuitions. Minor intuitions of a practical nature, pertaining to the personal self, seem to arise usually in the unconscious, and presumably pass to the left hemisphere of the brain for processing. Major intuitions of an abstract philosophical nature pertaining to the real self arise in the higher mind, enlightened by the buddhic principle, and are presumably handled initially by the right hemisphere, though the left will be called in to work out verbal expression. The lower and higher parts of the emotional nature may respectively also become involved in the two types of intuitional experience.

Such ideas have become more acceptable and "respectable" in recent decades. So distinguished a scientist as Sir Peter Medawar has written on this topic, notably in his *Induction and Intuition in Scientific Thought* (Medawar 1969). At a more spiritual level, Virginia Burden's book *The Process of Intuition; A Psychology of Creativity* (Burden 1987) may be noted. An alternative title might well be *Intuition as a Way of Life*.

LATERAL THINKING BY INDIVIDUALS AND GROUPS

Two variants on straightforward creative thinking may be mentioned. The first is what de Bono calls lateral thinking (de Bono 1985). Most people suppose that a problem should be tackled by stepwise logical thinking, proceeding vertically from problem to solution without error—but without originality. But often this direct attack fails. Appeals for insight also sometimes meet with no response and come to a dead end. At this stage, lateral thinking can profitably be tried. The attempt at a direct solution is firmly put out of the mind. Instead the mind is encouraged to browse at random in closely related areas, or even in distant ones. This way of thinking may seem chaotic and self-indulgent; but it differs from mere daydreaming in that it is guided, however loosely, and that the mind assumes an attitude of watchfulness, "listening" for any hint of relevance to the problem in hand. As de Bono points out, logic is a means for digging holes that get deeper and better; but that is useless if the hole is in the wrong place. Yet one is reluctant to waste the intellectual effort that has gone into digging that hole. Recourse to lateral thinking demands this sacrifice; it is the search for a new site. Rigidity of thinking needs to be set aside in favor of a free, fluidic approach. Not infrequently this kind of guided daydreaming does turn up a completely new approach to the original problem, leading to its eventual solution. Clearly, this is a technique for wooing the intuition.

The second variant is virtually lateral thinking done by a research group; it is called "brainstorming," and has been used particularly in some American universities and even business firms. Participants are encouraged to set aside their inhibitions and to come out with anything that occurs to them, however slight a connection it may seem to have with the problem in hand. The hope is that it will stimulate another member of the group to arrive at a more fruitful idea. Thus thoughts are battered around, until by joint effort a possible solution worthy of experimental testing is found. There is only one rule in brainstorming; nobody may criticize anything that is said, however useless or even preposterous it may seem at first hearing.

Earlier, in Chapter 9, I offered a criterion to distinguish recall of brain memories from reception from the unconscious mind. Brain memories flow into the mind on request, without effort or delay; impressions from the unconscious pop into the mind at inopportune moments when it is disengaged, blank, and thus momentarily in a receptive state. This criterion remains generally valid, but exceptions must be noted. With long experience, it is possible to cultivate a frame of mind, or rather an exalted state of consciousness, in which one is fully open to messages from the unconscious, including intuition or inspiration. These revelations then flow into the mind as if generated by one's own thinking, without hindrance or any sense of surprise. This is a condition well known to creative writers. It has been called "reverie" (Green and Green 1978), but probably a better term is that used by Whiteman, "continuous recollection" (Whiteman 1961). I recall that some fifty years ago, when I supposed that writing demanded a state of concentrated cerebration, I would sometimes be pulled up by a problem to which I saw no solution. A trick I then used was deliberately to break the concentration by unwrapping and chewing a toffee. During this interlude, the answer to my problem would often slip into my mind, with the usual "Eureka" sensation.

However the messages come, it does not seem possible in most instances to distinguish their source; they may come from some more or less impersonal reservoir, from one's own unconscious mind, or from a living or discarnate personal friend, guru, or guide. The exception is when they are accompanied by a "sense of presence" of the sender. This phenomenon is well attested in mystical writings.

CREATIVITY

Creativity is mainly an affair of the higher mind. What emerges may be given expression in writing, or alternatively in any art form. Or again there may be no overt expression beyond the remolding of one's own life, in the direction of greater efficiency or spirituality.

Creative thinking is essentially the enunciation and development of ideas received in flashes of intuitive insight. Clearly some preparation is needed. For a writer the theme is selected in advance, the "homework" is done by way of looking up what has already been written on the subject, and brooding upon it for some days or even longer. Logical thinking needs to be pursued to its limit. Only when this limit is reached and the mind falters and can make no further progress may intuition come to the rescue with fresh inspiration and comprehension.

Then an appointment is made with the "muse." One may say to oneself, "At 9:00 a.m. tomorrow I resolve to seek enlightenment on this matter." With faith born of previous experience, the creative thinker opens himself to the superconscious, and he can rely upon inducing the right conditions for the flow of insight. He will empty his mind of mundane thoughts and slip into a higher state of consciousness. Indeed, for the duration of this endeavor it is as well, if not imperative, for the entire personality to become subservient to the higher self; it should be quietly relegated to its proper place, as an agent of the true self. This can be an exhilarating yet humbling experience, which makes all the hard work seem worthwhile. This is what keeps a creative thinker going, joyfully. His work becomes better than it would otherwise have been—yet he can no longer claim it as wholly his own. Of course, great creative thinkers adopt this attitude naturally, without needing to analyze the situation. Any desire to dominate or to be assertive is a fatal barrier to intuition, as is an argumentative mind.

If one is a writer, he will prepare himself with pen and note pad, or sit down at the typewriter or word processor, fairly confident (though not cocksure!) of another fruitful session writing his book or recording whatever he gleans for future use. Alternatively of course, he may dictate the material to a secretary or tape recorder. It is always advisable to have writing materials or a recorder available, because intuitions are elusive; they come as wordless intimations, difficult for the memory to encode, and they tend to fade away wholly or in part. Until they are turned into concrete thoughts expressed in words, there is nothing much to hold on to. So they should always be recorded, even when one realizes that the only words one can find are no more than a travesty of the actual experience. They are better than nothing at all.

There is a second good reason for this recording step. While the mind struggles to retain the intuition in its original purity, it cannot receive further enlightenment. Writing frees it again, and further insight may then follow.

My personal experience is that I may brood over the subject for days or even weeks. From time to time relevant ideas flash into the mind, by day or night, sometimes already expressed in suitable words. Then I must hasten to jot them down before they are lost. When I come to do the actual drafting, I write or type rapidly for a while, then pause to mull over the next section, and so forth. The product is not the final version; it is revised a few days later; further insertions or alterations may suggest themselves at odd times. Final revisions are made when later chapters have been written.

This kind of experience is by no means unique, though each writer will have his own quirks. The best-selling novelist Catherine Cookson relates how she trusts her subconscious mind and creative imagination. She never works out a plot in advance, or makes any notes. First she decides on characters and places them in an environment, remembered or researched. Then she finds a beginning and an ending to the story, and starts dictating as the tale tells itself, so to speak. If it does not go smoothly, she "sleeps on it," and any difficulties sort themselves out.

Annie Besant, who was a brilliant lecturer, had a different technique. As she spoke, alternative versions of the next sentence would appear, as if in text, before her mind's eye, and she would select the best one. My wife is another person who seems habitually open to the unconscious mind. Once, in course of conversation, she made some wise remark. Then she stopped in surprise and said, "Oh, I didn't know that until I said it!"

Creativity can be expressed in many other ways. It is not essential to be especially gifted or highly trained. Anyone who so chooses and who puts his heart into it can display creativity in some manner, great or small, in ways that need not involve heavy expenditure. An obvious outlet is some form of art. Anyone who can draw should cultivate this talent, and possibly extend it to painting in watercolor or in oils or more exotic media. Such pursuits are avenues for creative self-expression, but may also effect release of stress or tension. Alternatives are molding, sculpture, or pottery. An extension is interior decorating. An individual or a couple may express their creativity by designing and producing a beautiful home, giving satisfaction to themselves and to friends. Some people learn to play a musical instrument; once moderate proficiency has been attained, attention can be devoted to the quality of performance and to interpretation of the music in one's individual style, which again brings out latent creativity. On a smaller scale, one may take up flower arranging. This can be quite inexpensive; a Japanese woman may spend an hour arranging a couple of flowers or twigs in the most expressive manner she can achieve.

Creative talents can be expressed outdoors too, for example in the creation of beautiful gardens containing plants well suited to the local soil and climate, artistically arranged to display blending and contrast of color and form. This is a pursuit of growing popularity, especially in the British Isles. Surprisingly perhaps, I would include sports, as well as athletics and dancing, as outlets for creativity. The pursuit of excellence in these and other fields is a splendid objective, but moderate competence adequate to permit the development of individual style can be very satisfying. Many activities that have to be performed anyhow, like cooking, are commonly regarded as tiresome chores. If they are done artistically, meticulously, and lovingly, then life becomes much more agreeable; the joy of creativity can be found in such simple tasks, however meager one's resources may be.

There remains another field, all too often neglected, through which creativity can be expressed—the cultivation of our own selves, outer and inner. We can look after the health, fitness, and appearance of our bodies. We can take care to dress neatly and appropriately, even elegantly, with becoming colors. A woman especially may thus enhance her beauty, so that she will feel good about herself and give much pleasure to others. But a more important area is the *inner* self, too often left to look after itself. Human nature *can* be changed, and the place to start is with our own. If we want to be loved, we must make ourselves lovable. Disagreeable habits can be curbed, agreeable ones cultivated. The character can be transformed, with diligent effort, until resplendence shines forth from our eyes. Then human relationships can become deeper, more meaningful and intense. Thus is creativity applied to supreme advantage.

Resumé

Intuition does not arise from one specific level of consciousness, but from whatever level is immediately beyond our usual span. Minor intuitions of a practical nature usually derive from the personal unconscious. For many people intuition represents an expansion of consciousness from the lower to the higher mind, which thinks in wordless ideas. More spiritual transcendental intuitions involve the buddhic principle. However, intuitions are not always right, due to transmission errors, so they should always be checked. Errors arise in formulating abstract revelations in concrete thoughts or words, or wishful thinking may masquerade as intuition. It may be sought but not commanded to appear. The mind needs to have been prepared thoroughly, to have exhausted the possibilities of logical thinking. Variants on straightforward creative thinking are de Bono's technique of lateral thinking and brainstorming in research groups. Intuitions usually enter the mind with a shock, the "Eureka experience"; but after long practice of creative thinking, they may flow in smoothly. Examples are given of the course of the creative process.

15

Disciplined Thinking: Biofeedback, Health, Yoga

Inhibit the modifications of the thinking principle.
Patanjali

From childhood onwards we accumulate possessions. At first they are toys we have been given, books, drawing books, pencils, and so forth. From time to time we parade our belongings and gloat over them. In later life we amass not only objects needed in the home, but all sorts of oddities that might come in handy sometime. Many homes are littered with necessities, ornaments, and junk. It is much the same with our thoughts. These too we treasure and hold on to; anything that interests us we automatically commit to memory. But we do this also with our worries and grievances, which would better be forgotten. These especially we tend to parade before the mind's eye, so that they grow in intensity and seeming importance. Eventually they present themselves unbidden for still another review, along with other memories of more pleasant and recent events. In short, most of us have minds that are cluttered and undisciplined; they are forever engaged in an "internal dialogue" that is mostly fruitless, and only occasionally produces a solution to one of our problems.

This internal chattering may continue after retiring for the night, in the form of insomnia. To cope with this situation, thousands of tons per annum of sleeping tablets are consumed. Most people accept this state as natural and unavoidable. But the situation is unnecessary; it could be averted by learning to control the mind. This may be a long and arduous task, but the rewards are immense. It is possible, though difficult, to cultivate an ordered, disciplined mind.

It might be said that mind control is the main object of the educational system, and to a degree this is so. At school in my young days we were taught assiduously the "three R's," reading, writing, and arithmetic, along with other subjects; our progress in memorizing the information was monitored by day-to-day tests and by periodic examinations, and laziness was duly punished. At secondary school the process continued, gradually becoming more specialized, and culminated in a university degree for those who continued that far. For the most part, it was a training in memory rather than thinking, though in mathemetics there were problems to be solved. I still recall my own enormous sense of release on learning that I had secured a good degree, and could stay on to do research in physical chemistry for a higher degree. At last, I reflected, I am no longer obliged to reproduce the thoughts of other men in order to pass exams; at last I am permitted to think creatively for myself about my research problems.

In the following half-century there have been a number of "progressive" experiments in teaching procedures, but many seem on the whole to have produced undesirable results. In many schools children are no longer expected to work hard, to apply themselves diligently to their tasks. This is considered "bad" for them, so they are only required to study whatever they find interesting and wish to learn. Boring topics like multiplication tables, grammar, and spelling are tackled only perfunctorily. Accordingly, too many children leave school unfit for employment except in the humblest and least exacting of jobs and needing calculators for even the simplest sums. It is true that learning is easier and is remembered better if it is found to be interesting. But the corollary to this is that methods of teaching need to be revised, to present even subjects regarded as dull in an interesting manner.

Another valid criticism is that now, as in my youth, the emotional needs of children are often ignored. Creativity may not be encouraged. The main objective in most schools is still to cram facts into minds regarded as empty, instead of developing faculties of feeling and thinking, inherently present in latent form from the start. In some youngsters these faculties burst forth and flourish regardless, and such gifted ones may have brilliant careers and lead happy lives.

Mind Control Methods

In later life, there are further opportunities to "improve the mind." Besides organized study, numerous commercial organizations offer courses in mind control, improving memory acquisition and recall with mnemonics, and so forth; in addition one can learn speed-reading and speed-writing. Alternately, one can learn how to delegate some of these tasks to computers, to avoid the need to stretch one's own mind. Many of these schemes are primarily for personal and commercial gain, directed towards greater earning or money-making potential, rather than mind development for its own sake or for altruistic ends. Moreover, all these schemes are incomplete and imperfect.

In any event, one learns to concentrate periodically in one's work, but in less demanding periods the mind is allowed to relapse into its former undisciplined state and to do just whatever it likes, mostly to daydream or to worry. There is little realization that this is an unsatisfactory state of affairs and that it is possible to take the mind in hand in a more fundamental fashion and to retrain it to become a disciplined and efficient servant of one's inner nature.

HEALTH: BIOFEEDBACK

When some progress has been made in mental control, it can be turned to good advantage for the promotion of bodily health. This can be done in two ways. In general "positive thinking" can be used to maintain the physical body in robust health and well-being. Specifically, it can be used, with or without the help of biofeedback techniques, to treat particular ailments. Our natural state is one of robust health, fitness, abundant vitality, and general well-being. If something approaching this condition already exists, it can be maintained and enhanced by disciplined thinking. The wrong approach is forceful *willing* of the body to stay well. A gentler approach is far more effective; the *imagination* is the proper tool to use. Just five minutes a day spent vividly imagining the body to be in perfect condition can work wonders.

Total faith in the power of thought is necessary, but a faltering faith may soon be strengthened by positive results. Other requisites are a sensible diet, adequate but not excessive in quantity, and regular exercise, vigorous but not too strenuous or prolonged. In addition, peace of mind is essential for perfect health. Life and work may be busy, stressful, and tiring, yet this need have no adverse effect on health. It is only when the stress is regarded as unbearable, as "getting the best of me," that it turns into harmful strain.

These are obviously counsels of perfection that we cannot all live up to all the time. When we fail, we may fall ill. First, at the mental and emotional levels we suffer from worry and resentment; then the physical body falls into line. Many illnesses, perhaps most, are psychosomatic, i.e. they are induced by sickness in the psyche. This can be true even for illnesses that have an "obvious" physical cause, such as viral and bacterial infections. These maleficent agents are about us all the time; some may even lie dormant within our bodies. Normally the body's immune system can effectively keep them at bay, but negative thoughts weaken this system, and we may fall victim to the infection. Some people may even unconsciously invite illness as a way to get a respite from intolerable tensions, though of course they would strenuously deny this. Instead they curse fate and throw the blame on someone who coughed or sneezed in their presence. But our secret desires are sometimes more powerful than our conscious ones. Constant vigilance and honest introspection are called for if we seek to be aware of all that goes on in our hearts and minds.

It is not claimed that all ill health is psychosomatic in origin. Some afflictions are genetically determined, e.g. inborn errors of metabolism. They can show up as birth defects or deformities and degenerative diseases that develop in later life. We can be poisoned by impurities in our food or in the environment, such as lead and other toxic elements. Also we may meet with crippling accidents. Positive thinking may not guard us from such misfortunes, but it can often be used to lessen their disabling effects. This is becoming recognized in orthodox physiotherapy; for example, there are techniques to open new neural pathways to replace others that have become paralyzed or otherwise ineffective.

When ill health does arise, from whatever real or supposed cause, it can be tackled in a variety of ways. Surgery is sometimes unavoidable. Orthodox medicine has an armory of drugs to treat specific conditions; there are antibiotics, analgesics, diuretics, tranquilizers. In addition, many alternative treatments are available, such as acupuncture, manipulative treatments, homeopathy, herbal remedies. Some practitioners claim that orthodox medicine tends to treat symptoms rather than underlying physical and mental conditions. In general, the alternative techniques tend to treat the whole sick individual rather than the specific manifestations of disease. The choice is bewildering, so most people just rely on their local general practitioner. Some relatively rare individuals accept full responsibility for their own health and well-being. They seek to live in harmony with nature and spiritual principles. If they nevertheless fall sick, they have faith in inner guidance to the healing technique best suited to their condition.

In this book it is appropriate to describe in more detail only those healing methods that rely primarily upon disciplined thinking. These methods capitalize upon and encourage the body's remarkable capacity for self-healing and regeneration of damaged tissues. Among them is the famous mantrum of Dr. Coue, "Every day in every way I am getting better and better and better." Christian Science works on similar lines. Such general pleas may well be supplemented by "talking to the body" with more specific requests for the rectification of faults that have developed. In later years particularly, limbs may be stiff or arthritic, muscles may become enfeebled; there may be a tendency to anemia, the heart may be faulty, and so on. So it is a good idea to spell out what improvements one would like the body to accomplish.

It is worthwhile to repeat each such request three

times, with concentrated intent; it is useless just to mumble the words without putting powerful thoughts into them. Also, once again, it must be insisted that faith in results is essential. Naturally one must be reasonable. Instant miracle cures *do* occur, but they are rare exceptions. Normally one is looking for slow, steady improvement; in extreme old age one may have to be content to halt or delay further deterioration. Results are impossible to quantify, but the growth of an abiding sense of well-being can be unmistakable, and the few remaining aches, pains, and disabilities can become unimportant and acceptable. That, at any rate, is my own experience at an age of over eighty, after a serious illness followed by some ten years of effort along these lines.

In appropriate conditions, such techniques can be enormously assisted and strengthened by biofeedback methods (Karliss and Andrews 1973). Biofeedback can be defined as a method of controlling a biological system by reinserting into it the results of past performance. Actually this is something we do all the time, without realizing it and without using any instruments. However, it can be done in a planned, deliberate manner. It is possible by thought-power or a change in behavior to bring about instant or fairly rapid results that can be measured by some appropriate instrument. Then the readings of the instrument are fed back to the subject, either by a dial reading or via some visual or audible signal. These signals provide instant encouragement to the subject and confirmation that he is doing the right things. This is important because often it is impossible to explain to the subject precisely what he needs to do. Moreover, even when he has done it correctly and has evoked the signal, the subject himself cannot state clearly what it was he did; often he just chanced upon the right behavior. But with the help of biofeedback signals, he can gradually learn the knack of making the right response. Even then it may remain inexplicable, because in some instances the right action involves taking over control of autonomic functions, formerly believed to be beyond deliberate control.

Some examples are clearly needed to expand and justify these remarkable claims. A prerequisite for any attempt to use disciplined thinking for healing purposes is relaxation of body and mind. As noted in Chapter 8, such relaxation is signalled by a dramatic change in brain rhythm from the busy, fast beta rhythm of normal brain activity to the slower alpha rhythm that marks the cessation of active thinking; in some instances, or with some individuals, a deeper state of relaxation is signalled by the still slower theta rhythm. These brain waves are usually monitored by an electroencephalogram that produces a continuous trace on a moving strip of paper; but for biofeedback purposes the various rhythms can be multiplied in frequency·so as to be presented as recognizably different musical tones. With practice these enable a subject to slip into the slower rhythms at will in a matter of minutes or even seconds, even though he may not be able to describe how he does it. As noted earlier, the ability to do this is a boon to people who lead stressful lives.

Another technique in biofeedback training is to teach the subject to warm his own hands. The usual procedure is to tape thermistors to a finger and to the brow as a control point. A meter registers the difference in temperature between the two points. The subject is usually told simply to imagine that his hands are getting warmer. He may imagine they are dipping into hot water or held before a fire, or he may suppose, more correctly, that a source of internal heat is warming them. What actually happens is that capillary blood vessels that have been constricted open up so that blood flows more freely in them close to the skin, so that the skin temperature rises. In a good subject temperature may rise as high as 95°F (36°C), only a few degrees below normal blood temperature. But the person does not need to know the exact mechanism or to think about it. Indeed it is not even necessary to tell him the objective of the test; he may be instructed simply to make the pointer on the meter move to the right.

This particular test is simple and usually works, even with skeptical subjects who initially believe it to be impossible. So it can be used to give the subject confidence in preparation for training in other techniques that seem even more improbable. But it is useful in itself; the subject may suffer from habitually cold hands, and may welcome a way of warming them when external sources of heat are not immediately available. A more subtle utility is the ability to cure or ameliorate migraine headaches. This condition is generally associated with elevated blood pressure in the brain; raising the temperature of the hands internally relieves this excessive pressure and so relieves the migraine.

Many people experience chronic anxiety states, often accompanied by habitual muscular tension. Simply teaching them to relax both body and mind can bring enormous relief, and this can be done very simply using biofeedback. Muscular tension can be monitored with an electromyogram. The readings are displayed to the subject, who is told he must try to keep them at low levels. He is also told to relax the muscles of the forehead; he can feel whether or not he has done this without instrumentation. An EEG machine can be used to monitor brain rhythms, and the subject must try to maintain alpha rhythm. The subject must accept the need for treatment and must be ready to cooperate, or nothing will be accomplished. Biofeedback is not a form of external treatment but merely training in self-help.

Moreover, the subject must not come to rely on repeated sessions in the laboratory; instead he must learn to recognize the knacks he uses to make the instruments register the required readings, and he must continue to use these regularly at home when he has no access to the machines.

Biofeedback training may help cure insomnia. Patients with heart and circulation problems can also be helped. The heartbeat can be registered with a cardio-tachometer; the readings can be analyzed by a computer, and the results fed to "traffic lights." Red signifies too fast, green too slow; amber signifies within normal range, and the patient must try to keep the light at amber. Blood pressure can also be monitored and the readings can be displayed. It is claimed that the common complaint of hypertension can be ameliorated by the patient's conscious actions in response to the readings. This possibility is of course contrary to the teachings of orthodox physiology. Elmer and Alyce Green (1978), pioneers of biofeedback training, wisely conclude that for self-regulation of any kind to be effective, it must become a way of life. Improved health lies in learning to coordinate the conscious and the unconscious so that they work together for the well-being of the individual.

There is a lot of evidence that even malignant conditions may respond to faith and thought power, notwithstanding that the only biofeedback available is the feeling of greater health that slowly prevails. Among the pioneers are Carl and Stephanie Simonton of Fort Worth, Texas. They are both medically qualified, and their approach is to use orthodox treatments for cancer, such as radiation and powerful drugs, but also to persuade their patients to use controlled imagination to destroy any remaining cancerous cells. They may thus prevent the development of the metastasis that so often follows such treatment. But numerous other practitioners have used similar techniques successfully as an *alternative* to orthodox treatment. Orthodox doctors tend to brush aside such cures by faith healing as "spontaneous remissions." But what do they really mean by "spontaneous remission"? The term is used for any recovery that occurs without any cause they consider valid. Thus the term is really synonymous with "miracle," for things do not happen spontaneously, i.e. by sheer chance, in nature; there has to be some cause. Whenever such cases are followed up diligently, it is found that the patient made a trip to Lourdes, or fellow members of his church joined in prayers for his recovery, or he got in touch with some group with belief that thought power and faith can cure even the dreaded cancer. However irrational such happenings may appear to the materialistically minded, the facts are sufficiently well established to merit general recognition.

YOGA SYSTEMS

For millennia mind control has been practiced for impersonal, spiritual ends. It has taken the form of meditation, yoga, or prayer and has been available in monasteries and mystery schools in the East, the Near East, Europe, and elsewhere. These practices fell somewhat into disrepute with the advance of material science; but they are now coming into their own again, as more and more people come to realize values beyond those of science.

The Eastern methods have become fairly well known in the West, for example, through translations of *The Yoga Sutras* of Patanjali, written around 600 B.C. Patanjali is brief and blunt: "Inhibit the modification of the thinking principle." So too is the Mexican Indian "sorcerer" don Juan, who commends his pupil Carlos Castaneda to "stop the internal dialogue." Translations of Hindu and Buddhist scriptures are also available, and numerous commentaries have been made by theosophical and other writers.

The mind—or is it the brain?—is seldom quiet and at rest. Generally, one thought just leads on by association to another, and yet another. This is "lateral thinking" gone to waste because it is without purpose. Only a still, silent mind is conducive to inner peace and harmony, to the spiritual union which is the meaning and the objective of Raja Yoga.

These yoga systems are not altogether suited to Western temperaments, and alternative Western traditions are also to be found. I shall not enlarge on these beyond heartily commending a recent two-volume work by Caitlin and John Matthews, called *The Western Way*. The first volume is entitled *The Native Tradition* and the second *The Hermetic Way* (Matthews 1985, 1986). These books, along with their 700 references, constitute an adequate guide for anyone wishing to study or to practice the Western disciplines, whether individually or by group ritualistic ceremonies.

This is again not the place to expound other yoga systems in detail. There are plenty of books available; recommended for beginners are those by V. W. Slater (1965, 1966) and for the more deeply involved, Taimni's translation of and commentary on Pantanjali (1975). Briefly, these include exhortations to lead a sober, unselfish, disciplined life, to forego attachment to earthly delights, and to meditate regularly.

This word "meditation" is used in a general sense, covering all three of its stages, and more specifically the second stage. The first stage is *concentration*, in which the mind is focused steadily upon a single object or idea, without digressing or wandering. The second stage is *meditation*, in which the mind is allowed to digress from the object or idea, but only to all its properties, aspects, or associations, thinking around and about the chosen subject without ever wandering from it altogether onto an alien train of thought. The third stage is *contemplation*, a state of superconsciousness, ecstacy, or mystical experience which is beyond emotion or thought, even beyond self. It is the state of union with the Source of all, the objective of Raja Yoga.

Books on Raja Yoga (e.g. Slater 1965) tend to treat contemplation as a mystical state. Taimni (1975) explains that the Sanskrit word "samadhi" covers a wide range of contemplative states at mental, buddhic, and atmic levels. Whiteman (1986) avoids the word "contemplation" altogether and translates "samadhi" as "recollection." He distinguishes between active recollection and continuous recollection, both being states below mystical grades. Western religious works tend to accept the lower reaches of Taimni's range as meriting the term "contemplation." This is what I should regard as brooding, or dwelling upon an understanding, or alternatively as a state of intense spiritual love.

The whole procedure might be summed up as cultivating the art of maintaining an empty mind and a full heart. The mind is empty only of *extraneous* thoughts. It is filled entirely with thoughts on the chosen topic, and eventually consciousness passes beyond mind altogether. The heart is full of pure love for the One, the Source of all, and for all creatures.

Physiological Correlates of Meditation

Physiologically, in meditation the body is in a unique state, differing from any other waking or unconscious condition, as meditation has specific physiological correlates. Among the more detailed studies are those made by Wallace and Benson (1972) on thirty-six subjects who followed the meditation system called "Transcendental

Meditation" devised by Maharishi Mahesh Yogi. All subjects during their meditation periods went into what was called a "hypometabolic state": that is to say, their condition differed in many respects from that of sleep and also from hypnosis, and nearly all metabolic functions measured were depressed below normal waking levels. Specifically, both the rate of respiration and the volume transpired were diminished; oxygen consumption and carbon dioxide exhaled were both some 20 percent below normal. There was a slight increase in blood acidity, but the level of lactate in the blood fell markedly, by almost half in some subjects. The heart rate also fell by about three beats per minute. Skin resistance rose fourfold. Another interesting finding was increased blood flow in the forearms, presumably due to dilation of blood vessels. It is highly significant that many of these changes are the exact opposite of those that occur in anxiety states. In particular, high blood levels of lactate and low skin resistance are characteristic concomitants of anxiety.

The authors emphasized that this pattern of changes is unique and is not paralleled in more than a few particulars in any other state of consciousness. In sleep, for example, oxygen consumption does diminish, but only after several hours. The acidity and carbon dioxide level in the blood both rise, but this is due to shallow respiration and decreased ventilation and not to changes in metabolism as in meditation. Skin resistance rises in sleep, but much less than during meditation. In sleep the brain shows high-voltage slow waves at 10-12 per second (spindle waves) plus weaker waves at various frequencies, quite different from the meditation pattern. In hypnosis there is no change in the oxygen consumption, and other signs alter in a manner that depends entirely on the suggestions made by the hypnotist.

In operant conditioning by rewards it is possible to increase or decrease heart rates or to alter other specific autonomic functions. In meditation, on the other hand, there is no reward (except, one might say, the serenity induced), and there is a general integrated group of responses, not just a specific one. The changes are complex and are related to a highly relaxed state; in all respects they are opposite to the changes induced by the "fight or flight" or "defense alarm" reactions to stress or an alarming challenge which instantly induces a hypermetabolic state, a condition in which the rates of many metabolic functions are increased. This is a situation that arises all too frequently in the busy world in an exaggerated and anachronistic fashion; our health is apt to suffer from the succession of arousals of racing metabolism—automatic reactions which often greatly exceed what the situation really calls for. Meditation is the exact opposite, and the authors speculate that the hypometabolic state it induces could very well have clinical applications to counterbalance the harm done by frequent excessive arousals.

This kind of work leaves one in no doubt that meditation is a real and unique state of consciousness that can easily be recognized by numerous objective physical signs. Moreover, besides the control of mind and emotions and conditioning of the personality towards serenity—which its advocates claim as advantages—there are good scientific reasons to suggest that meditation also improves physical health. The investigators, who themselves practiced "TM," were actively discouraged from working with practitioners of other systems of meditation. But earlier work suggests that anyone who meditates successfully will show these same physiological correlates. In this account I have deliberately placed the words "transcendental meditation" in quotation marks, to emphasize that *all* meditation is transcendental.

What then is meant by "transcendental"? This is a question that is seldom posed, and even less often are specific answers offered. Clearly it involves a progressive process of lifting the span of consciousness. We may picture the situation as a ladder with its upper end firmly attached to a heavenly skyhook. As we climb, we draw up the lower rungs behind us, i.e. we transcend them. One significant stage is transcendence of the personality, so that consciousness is centered in the individuality or spiritual nature.

There is one fundamental first step, without which no meditation can succeed. As argued elsewhere in this book, transcendence is of the brain, that possessive, domineering organ that claims our attention constantly; until its stranglehold is broken we can make no progress. This situation poses a dilemma for the unfortunate materialist. For him the brain is already the top of the ladder; so in principle it *cannot* be transcended. If it were, there would be nothing left—consciousness would cease. This really does seem a shortsighted attitude, in the light of the realms beyond, displayed in the diagrams of Chapter 12.

A review by Jonathan B. B. Earle of Medford, Massachusetts (Earle 1981) concerns brain hemispheric activity in meditation. The author concedes that the objective of most kinds of meditation is to transcend thinking. Nevertheless, electrical activity in the brain continues. The published evidence, supported by the author's own work, suggests that meditation leads to closely coordinated activity in both hemispheres. I have pointed out earlier (Chapter 7) that this is a desirable condition worth cultivating.

Returning to Eastern yoga systems, it is clear that Raja Yoga is not *merely* a system of mind control; it is a whole new way of life. To avoid confusion, it should be mentioned that a different yoga system, Hatha Yoga, has become more widely known in the West; in fact it is often called just "yoga," as if it were the *only* system.

It concentrates on breath control, bodily postures, and exercises; mind control is only a minor part. Most of the Hindu yoga systems tend to be life-negating practices; they regard the whole manifested world and the physical body as relatively useless and illusory. They are suited to those with a taste for the monastic life, or for the high-caste Indian who traditionally retired to a mountain cave to meditate in the last quarter of his life. Such practices do not fit with a Western way of life, and tend to be regarded as "escapist." However, some Westerners find themselves attracted to the Zen Buddhist system.

YOGA FOR THE WEST

Some years ago when surveying the field, I lighted upon a modernized yoga discipline called "Integral Yoga," adapted from Tantric Hinduism by Sri Aurobindo and his disciple Haridas Chaudhuri (1965), an Indian who lived and worked in California. This is a joyous, positive, life-affirming system, which seeks to purify and upgrade the personality and the body, to make them worthy channels for spiritual power. It is called "Integral Yoga" because it is a synthesis of the best features of all other yoga disciplines, and seeks to avoid the unbalanced development that some of them induce.

The negative attitude is the world-negating approach, exemplified by Patanjali (and also by some Christian traditions, especially those of the puritanical sects, whose advice is to turn one's back on the world, the flesh and the devil). According to most Eastern systems, one must seek the life of the spirit, which means to deny and subjugate the personality: it is impermanent, it errs by clinging to illusions, and one must instead cultivate the spiritual nature. The objective of this approach is to reach Nirvana, and to stay in that state, basking in eternal bliss, so to speak.

An example of a nation that has tended to take this negative path is India. Few in the Western world would welcome this negative way. The West is deeply committed to the material world. But idealists in the West would welcome the idea that inner understanding should be channelled towards improving the sorry state of the world. The world is not irredeemable; it can be, must be, and will be redeemed in due time. So Integral Yoga is for those who do not want to opt out and merely arrange for their own personal salvation. They want to play their small parts towards the liberation of the whole human race, by being in the world, though not of the world. Integral Yoga looks forward to a unique world order, ruled not by materialistic values, but by spiritual ones.

The practice of Integral Yoga involves integration at three levels: 1) psychic, 2) cosmic, and 3) existential. Psychic integration means the harmonization of different aspects of the personality such as the conscious and unconscious, and the discovery of the higher individuality. Cosmic integration means realization and acceptance of the fact that the personal psyche and the cosmos are inseparable aspects of one concrete reality. Existential integration means uniting with the ultimate, timeless ground of existence. The Eternal is the most fundamental dimension of existence—but not the only one. The Eternal is pure transcendence, the peace of the mystic. But Being is also manifested in time as evolution and history. Mystical union with Being can be static or dynamic. Affirming the dynamic aspect, Integral Yoga brings mysticism back to earth; its objective is to become a *practical* mystic. With experience, the mystic acquires a working union with the divine. He becomes a dynamic, creative personality. But ascent to the heights is not the ultimate objective; it needs to be supplemented by descent and fuller affirmation.

Briefly, the objectives of Integral Yoga are striving for excellence and dedicated living for service in the world. These are, of course, ideals that any altruistic person might set for himself. But they may be achieved more effectively by yoga practices, and Integral Yoga is perhaps the kind best suited to Western man. Paradoxically, this transpersonal approach, ceasing to cultivate earthly pleasures and ambitions, leads in practice to a stronger personality and to increased efficiency in handling mundane affairs; indeed, it is more effective than direct striving for such goals. Moreover, one has peace of mind as a bonus—the best of both worlds in fact, though one will have outgrown the taste for the more earthy pleasures.

RÉSUMÉ

The normal "resting" state of the mind and brain is one of fruitless chattering to itself about worries and memories. The whole education process demands some control of thinking by way of concentration on the subject and memorizing facts. But between work periods, the brain reverts to the internal dialogue. Systems of mind control and memory training are commercially available; their purpose too often is competitive personal advantage. Disciplined thinking can be used to promote and maintain bodily health and well-being. To this end and for the treatment of various ailments, biofeedback techniques are valuable. Examples are provided. Even malignant conditions may respond to faith and thought power. Mind control for transpersonal, altruistic ends has been taught for millennia in yoga and mystery schools. The physiological correlates of meditative states are described. *All* meditation is transcendental; first the brain, then the mind is transcended, leading to contemplation and the mystical experience. Most Indian yogas are life-negating systems, not well suited to the Western temperament. The Western Hermetic tradition may be followed, or a modern life-affirming positive synthesis of Eastern yogas called Integral Yoga is commended.

16

Mystical Consciousness

Seeking nothing, he gains all;
Foregoing self, the Universe grows "I."
Sir Edwin Arnold

In this concluding chapter, it seems appropriate to contemplate conditions wherein normal discursive thinking is wholly transcended. In mystical consciousness, debate and argument seem to fall back in shame and amazement, to be displaced by silent contemplation of Plato's trio, truth, goodness, and beauty. Yet in this mystical state, quiet reflection upon the self-evident understanding that is reached is certainly possible. So this condition might perhaps be regarded as the apotheosis of thinking. It has often been said, in this book and elsewhere, that at the buddhic and higher levels mind (as well as brain) is transcended. This claim must now be qualified in some degree. That which is transcended is both concrete and abstract thinking *as we know it in human experience.* At higher levels there is and always has been Cosmic Mind or Cosmic Intelligence. This may be held to predate all physical life forms, as I pointed out in *Intelligence Came First* (Smith 1975). It is also noteworthy that Wilber (1977) uses the term "Mind" (with a capital "M") to name all levels beyond human mentation.

The term "mystical experience" has been used in earlier chapters to denote an exalted state of consciousness. In this chapter it will be considered in greater depth. In journalistic usage, the term "mystical" has been so far debased as to be employed in an almost derisory sense, for example as synonymous with "mysterious" or "mythical." Some people refuse to accept that it exists at all, except perhaps as a pathological condition. Again (and deplorably in my view) the term "mystic" is often used of somebody who is *interested in* mysticism, but has not had the experience himself. Mystical experience lies far beyond any kind of lower psychism, mediumship, or out-of-the-body experiences as commonly understood, meaning excursions into the duplicate world that resembles the physical (see Chapter 12). However, this state can be used effectively as a jumping-off point for higher levels, including the mystical.

R. Bucke, writing over eighty years ago, estimated the proportion of Westerners who have known what he calls "cosmic consciousness" to be around one in a million (Bucke 1961). This may have been an underestimate. In any event the proportion is without doubt higher now, possibly ten to a hundred per million. However, it is more meaningful to assess the prospects for a self-selected group, for example potential readers of this book. Most of them will be able to recall some experiences of ecstasy, uplift, or exaltation. These may be initiated by beauty of nature or art, music, religious services, "falling in love," and so forth. Possibly around a third of this group will know the greater exaltation of premystical experience, and a significant percentage will attain authentic mystical states.

This is important because mystics have a dispropor-
tionate influence in the world; they tend to evoke
mystical or exalted states in others. Some write books
or engage efficiently in altruistic activities. Those who
just live out their lives quietly radiate joy and good will;
they sweeten the "psychic atmosphere," and are recognized as persons with whom one can share one's problems and be comforted.

The description of the nature of mystical experience
given by Bucke, in the somewhat florid style of his
period, has often been taken as a model.

> I was in a state of quiet, almost passive enjoyment,
> not actually thinking, but letting ideas, images, and
> emotions flow of themselves, as it were, through my
> mind. All at once, without warning of any kind, I
> found myself wrapped in a flame-colored cloud. For
> an instant I thought of fire, an immense conflagra-
> tion somewhere close by in that great city; the next,
> I knew that the fire was within myself. Directly after-
> wards there came upon me a sense of exultation, of
> immense joyousness accompanied or immediately
> followed by an intellectual illumination impossible
> to describe. Among other things, I did not merely
> come to believe, but I saw that the universe is not
> composed of dead matter, but is, on the contrary, a
> living Presence; I became conscious in myself of eter-
> nal life. It was not a conviction that I would have
> eternal life, but a consciousness that I possessed eter-
> nal life then; I saw that all men are immortal; that
> the cosmic order is such that without any peradven-
> ture all things work for the good of each and all; that
> the foundation principle of the world, of all worlds,
> is what we call love; and that the happiness of each
> and all is in the long run absolutely certain. The vi-
> sion lasted a few seconds and was gone; but the
> memory of it and the sense of the quality of what it
> taught has remained during the quarter of a century
> which has since elapsed. I know that what the vision
> showed was true. I had attained to a point of view
> from which I saw that it must be true. That view,

that conviction, I may say that consciousness, has never, even during periods of the deepest depression, been lost.

By way of contrast, this may well be followed by the observations of a living scientist and mystic, Michael Whiteman (1961).

There is no possibility of mistaking a fully mystical state for a psychical one, on the score of either intelligibility or reality. Psychical states may indeed seem far more real than physical states, as if one had for the first time become really awake, but neither physical nor psychical states bear any comparison, as regards intelligibility, reality and *a priori* value, with mystical states.

Intuition nowadays is regarded as a fairly common experience; but mysticism is, so to speak, the next step on the spiritual ladder and is much less common. It is hard to explain in words; those who have known it do not need to read about it, and those who have not may not be much wiser from reading. In lesser exalted states, or expansions of consciousness as they are sometimes called, buddhi is involved, but not to the exclusion of the lower nature; in these states buddhi is playing through the mind or is reflected in feelings. An entire book has been written about ecstasy by Marghanita Laski (Laski 1961), and yet it hardly touches upon true mystical experience. Both intuition and mystical experience involve the love-wisdom-truth of buddhi: in intuition these qualities are illuminating the higher mind, while the mystic experiences them directly. To put it differently, there are two ways of knowing: at the mental level the self is studying the external world, but at the buddhic level knowing is by direct identification. This latter leads to self-evident knowledge of reality, to ultimate spiritual understanding and sensitivity.

Another helpful distinction is that intuitions characteristically come in a flash of insight. Mystical (and some premystical) experiences are more prolonged; they may start suddenly, though sometimes there is a preceding sense of expectancy, then they persist for minutes at least, sometimes much longer, before fading gradually into a long-lasting memory of the event. Further distinction lies in the quality of the revelation. An intuition usually conveys the answer to a specific question or to some area of puzzlement in thinking. The response may be surprising, but we already knew in what category of knowledge it would lie. It may nevertheless produce a profound effect in scientific thought. Mystical experiences, on the other hand, can bring wholly unexpected understanding of great spiritual profundity and broader generality, altogether of superior caliber.

As William James put it in *The Varieties of Religious Experience* (1961):

> This overcoming of all the usual barriers between the individual and the Absolute is the great mystic achievement. In mystic experience we become aware of our Oneness. This is the everlasting and triumphant mystical tradition, hardly altered by difference in clime or creed.

As Bucke also indicated, the mystic achieves a level of consciousness beyond the reach of most of us. His inmost divine nature becomes united with the Universal. He realizes himself to be one with all creation, one with the entire manifested universe at all levels; he perceives it no longer as an external observer but from within himself as an integral part of the whole. It is quite impossible to communicate the experience itself, for it is entirely beyond the realm of our inescapably dualistic thinking and language. An account of sorts can be written, and it may be quite moving, but the transcendent grandeur of the event itself is lost in the telling. Duality is so deeply ingrained that we are seldom aware of it, or even that any alternative might be possible. We accept totally a division into self and not-self, "I" versus "you" or "it." We are prisoners of the transitive verb which demands a subject and object. "I like you"; "He detests me"; "I own this." All this is part of our every-day world from which we rarely even wish to escape. But deep down, humanity is dimly aware that it is desirable and possible to escape from this divisive state into a condition in which you and I, he and it, are components of a glorious unity.

This is the state realized in mystical experience. It is not that there are two different or parallel worlds. There is only one world, but never before have we seen it whole. We have been caught up in our egocentric view—a false and illusory one, as ancient Indian scriptures assert. Even the attempt to hold a mystical experience in memory automatically converts it into thoughts, and these are thoughts *about* the experience, not the actual event itself. So each recipient transduces his vision in his own unique manner, colored and limited by his habitual thought patterns. A thousand such would not suffice to contain all that was given. They would all be different, yet sufficiently alike for their source to be recognized, at least by another mystic.

Music may be used to illustrate the idea of incommunicability. One may find rich enjoyment and spiritual meaning in listening to a late Beethoven quartet. One can talk about this to a musical friend and convey something of one's feelings. The better musically educated they both are, the more successful will be the attempt. But it is a poor substitute for listening to the music itself. Moreover, the words would convey nothing whatever to one born deaf, and little to one who does not like classical music.

We must not expect mystical revelation to provide ready-formulated scientific truths. The mystic himself must convert the experience, as best he can, into thoughts and language; in this endeavor he can only succeed if he is well-trained in science, and if his mind is well prepared to receive the revelation. Both approaches are needed; there is no short cut. Inspiration comes only to those who have earned it. Moreover, scientists are unable to make use of revelations formulated only in vague and general terms. Mystics sometimes wonder why their wondrous visions do not transform the world. I had the impression that Krishnamurti, for example, was permanently disappointed in this manner. The world needs *practical* visionaries who can translate revelations into effective action, as well as those who encourage others by showing the truth.

DEFINITION OF MYSTICISM

Mysticism is difficult to define, and few precise definitions are to be found in the literature. Bearing in mind that the art or science of mysticism must be clearly distinguished from the actual experience of mystical states of consciousness, the definition by Whiteman (1961) seems acceptable: "The study of everything nonphysical, the facts and their relationship being known by the *self-evidence* of direct observation and not by reasoning or speculation. Mysticism also includes what it is to be a mystic. . . ." This definition may seem at first glance to be rather broadly based and to include what I specifically excluded as being outside the scope of mystical *experience*. Closer study, however, shows that it is in fact very precisely formulated and limited. It states that not only mystical but also psychic realms can be studied by *direct observation* from a mystical state, a level at which facts automatically become self-evident. Thus the psychic realms can be studied in two distinct ways, which differ subtly in their scope. Psychics who are not mystics can observe them with their psychic faculties in a manner that is an extension of normal scientific methodology. That is to say, observations can be made and experiments can be performed, and the results can be recorded as a sort of natural history of these inner realms. But any explanations and meanings can only be derived by normal scientific procedures, i.e., by inference, intuition, hypothesis, and deduction.

Conclusions reached in these ways are fallible and may be overturned by deeper insights. As noted in Chapter 11, some degree of divine unity persists throughout all realms. It is this situation that the experienced mystic can exploit in his studies. He can, as it were, perceive the lower realms in the light of his mystical union, so that he can garner not merely cold facts, but some understanding of them, such understanding being self-evident and not fallible. The few pioneers who can operate in this manner afford a glimpse of a new methodology that will become available to scientists of the future.

Assessment of Mystical Experience

Despite the transcendental quality of mystical experience, it is entirely possible to study such states in a scientific manner. Some confusion has been created, however, when this has been attempted by those who have not themselves achieved authentic mystical experience but would like to believe that they had. The characteristic features are listed by Bucke (1961). His criteria will not be detailed here, but they may be illustrated by his views on two famous Americans: he thought that Walt Whitman was a true mystic, but that Emerson fell just short of that attainment. James offered four criteria (James 1961). The first is ineffability: "The subject of its contents cannot be given in words; it follows from this that its quality must be directly experienced. It cannot be imparted or transferred to others." His second criterion is noetic quality: "Although so similar to states of feeling, mystical states seem to those who experience them to be also states of knowledge. They are states of insight into depths of truth not plumbed by the discursive intellect." The third is transiency, and the fourth passivity: "When the characteristic sort of consciousness once has set in, the mystic feels as if his own will were in abeyance, and indeed sometimes as if he were grasped and held by a superior power."

James's criteria must be amended somewhat in the light of later studies. Mystical experience is indeed transcendental and incommunicable *in itself*. But a language of mysticism has emerged by which it can be *described* consistently in words easily intelligible to other mystics. They may still puzzle nonmystics, but at least they convey the reality of the experience and the fact that it is shared by a number of mystics. The aspect of transiency has been mentioned earlier. The duration is certainly longer than that of intuition, and indeed the state may eventually become nearly permanent. The term "passivity" could be misleading; it means only that self-will is blocked off; the spiritual nature is not passive, but on the contrary is intensely active "in obedience to the Source" (Whiteman 1961).

Whiteman was probably the first to propose a workable scheme to quantify the "quality" of both psychic and mystical experiences. To do this effectively, he analyzed personal or recorded accounts word by word in respect to six characteristics. Points are then allotted

Legend:

The three "degrees" of separation, and likewise of "undeveloped" and "borderline" types of separative experience. The total of points is called the General Index of Reality (GIR).

GIR			
	0 - 3 points:	*Undeveloped* types	
	4 - 5 points:	*Borderline* types	
	6 - 8 points:	First-degree or *Psychical* Separations	
	9 - 11 points:	Second-degree or *Premystical* Separations	
	12 - 16 points:	Third-degree or *Mystical* Separations	

Synopsis of Method of Assessment

Factor	Rating Scheme
R: *Intrinsic Reality* Sense of ultimates, logical priority, life-fullness, substance, tangibility, vivid participation.	0. no objective control or reflection. 1. some dreamlike or imaginative quality, reflection and attempts at control. 2. more "real" than the physical, as regards participation and substance; free observation. 3. strong participation, sense of substance and pin-pointed objectivity.
V: *Vertical Recollection* Openness to higher direction, including moral choice, guidance, and higher significance; "obedience".	0. complete lack. 1. some awareness of moral choice or guidance. 2. continuity of latent obedience. 3. manifest obedience to the Source.
H: *Horizontal Recollection* Openness to rational continuity, including memory of and comparisons with the physical state.	0. severe lack. 1. fairly good. 2. complete openness to comparisons.
I: *Integration* Integration and joy; transformation; poise, transcendence of emotionality, excitement and fear.	0. unpleasant or indifferent. 1. beginnings of a higher freedom. 2. a first integration and release from physical habits of thought; distinct improvement in bodily form. 3. transformation to "proper form".
P: *Personal Communion* Intercommunication of thought, feeling and impression of character; openness to instruction; selfless and loving identification.	0. no person seen, or only dreamlike or "lay" figures. 1. beginnings of objective knowledge of other minds, with communication of thought and feeling. 2. clear and direct intelligible communication. 3. communion in loving identification and interchange of wisdom.
M: *Continuity of Memory*	0. no memory on return (only comes later). 1. no complete break, but some difficulty or vagueness of recall. 2. memory continues vividly, as by perpetuation of the interior state, in detail and without a break.

From J. M. H. Whiteman, *The Meaning of Life,* Gerrards Cross England: Colin Smythe, 1986. Reproduced by permission of the author.

with a rating scheme. The total of points is called the "General Index of Reality" (GIR), and the quality of the event is judged to fall into one of five grades according to the score. Thus nine to eleven points indicates a premystical experience, and the fully mystical state requires a score of eleven plus to sixteen points. For effective use, the scheme really needs the fuller description that Whiteman provides, but Table 1 (reproduced from his book) gives a clear exposition of its scope (Whiteman 1986).

It is worth emphasizing that another person's experience can be assessed only from his own account of it. Strictly, therefore, it is the report that is being judged, not the experience itself. If scoring is performed sensitively, preferably by a mystic and not in mechanistic fashion, it is possible to gauge what the writer is trying to convey, and a reasonably fair judgment can be made.

The subject may, however, be a little confused and overwhelmed by the event, and may fail to do it full justice. An amusing example is provided by the two versions of Bucke's famous experience, which completely changed his life, and among other consequences led to the compilation of his book *Cosmic Consciousness*. His first account, quoted earlier in this chapter, is the original version published in a privately-circulated pamphlet, but preserved for posterity as it was quoted by James. Whiteman rates this at about 12 points on his GIR scale, which ranks it as fully mystical. But in his book, written much later, Bucke gives a revised and shortened account, which Whiteman rates at only 11 points, i.e., premystical only.

ATTAINMENT OF MYSTICAL CONSCIOUSNESS

The next stage of our enquiry into mysticism should bear on instructions on how to achieve this elusive state.

Unfortunately, this is even more difficult to convey than is the nature of the experience. First, there are two warnings to mention. Before embarking upon the quest, it is well to consider whether, if successful, the experience would really be welcomed. Mystical consciousness is not to be courted lightly. It can be a truly awful experience. I choose this word "awful" with full intent, but in its literal sense; it is an experience full of awe. As St. Augustine said, "I tremble both with love and with horror." In prospect, this plunge into an unknown realm can seem terrifying, to an extent that inhibits the effort. Even after having been there once or twice, one may shrink back into the comforting personality and be afraid to try again.

Yet if one does overcome these inhibitions, the experience is usually one of overwhelming bliss, almost too great to be borne. At the time, it does not matter if there is no return to normal life. But in retrospect, again it may be unsettling and catastrophic, especially if it came before one was well prepared. It carries with it imperative demands, to re-evaluate cherished beliefs, to change habits. The personality may not be ready, and conflicts may ensue. One may revert to worldly ambitious ways, but in quiet moments one may suffer shame from the memory of one's secret understanding. So sooner or later one must forego the freedom to do whatever one likes with no feeling of guilt. Sacrifices must be made, but the (otherworldly) rewards are great for those who are ready to receive them, as the words of St. Theresa testify:

> "God establishes himself in the interior of this soul in such a way, that when she returns to herself, it is wholly impossible for her to doubt that she has been in God, and God in her. This truth remains so strongly impressed on her that, even though many years should pass without the condition returning, she

> can neither forget the favor she has received, nor doubt its reality."

The second warning is not to try shortcuts; there are none. But it has been strongly suggested, sincerely though mistakenly, that genuine mystical states might be attained by the use of psychedelic drugs such as LSD or psilocybin. Such agents can certainly induce psychic states. Don Juan used "sacred mushrooms" and other plants to this end as part of the training of his pupil Carlos Castaneda. Others, for example Pahnke (Pahnke 1969), believed that in the right set and setting, with suitable preparation to induce the right mood, a drug (psilocybin) could confer true mystical experience.

For some years I was disposed to accept these claims. I argued that subjects are held back from entering this state by inability to let go of inhibitions (see later) and that the drug might loosen them up and overcome such inhibitions. So it does, but the ensuing visions fall well short of the fully mystical condition. Pahnke was using insufficiently stringent criteria for a mystical experience. The matter was finally settled for me by Irina Tweedie's book *The Chasm of Fire* (Tweedie 1979). Having entered the mystical state a few times under the guidance of her guru, she later tried LSD and found that the state it induced was far inferior to that of mystical consciousness following meditation.

One can live in such a manner as to put oneself in line, so to speak, for mystical enlightenment. Regular deep meditation helps, or being in the company of mystics, or reading their works. One cannot set out to practice mysticism, which comes by grace, not on demand, but it is possible to invite the experience. As Whiteman says: "The supreme purity and power cannot be reached by effort, for that would prevent detachment. In mystical language, it must be "infused."

The discipline he advocates may seem frightening in

its intensity. It includes: continuous exercise of recollection, complete detachment from all demands of the personal self, elimination of bad habits and desires, or preconceived ideas and prejudices (fixations). Other requirements are steadiness, serenity, undemanding love, and obedience. Yet after one has been dedicated to the spiritual life for some years, these disciplines come to be regarded merely as sensible adjustments to one's behavior pattern, needing only to be perfected and made habitual. The serenity and peace of mind induced by these observances is ample reward for the effort required.

Moreover, I suggest that these are attainments needed for *regular* admissions to the mystical state. It is clear from published reports that many people have an isolated experience long before their spiritual development has progressed that far. This may come in a moment of especial serenity, or in response to some powerful spiritual stimulus. Such disclosures might be regarded as premature, but any such judgment must be rejected as impertinent. The revelation, conferred by grace, may be intended to inspire or encourage the recipient, or to guide him in some altruistic endeavor that is required of him. The perceptive reader will recognize that I write from personal experience.

I can offer three simple analogies to the actual manner by which one gains entrance to the mystical state. They are learning to swim, going to sleep, and the out-of-body experience. Each of these events has three stages which can be detected by careful self-analysis. They are:

(a) letting go of something familiar and trusted;
(b) a leap into the unknown;
(c) release into a new world with an experience of joy.

Swimming is a homely analogy. One can learn *about* swimming on dry land. One can practice the strokes lying across a narrow table or pretend to swim hopping on one leg. One can splash about in shallow water to gain confidence. But none of this *is* swimming. In order to swim, one must pluck up courage to let go of every solid support. It is necessary to launch oneself into this new medium—water—and that is the leap. Then one is really swimming, and that is the joyous release from the familiarity of land. This first successful attempt is a great experience, a new skill learned never to be forgotten. But it required that brave step of letting go.

Similarly, sleep is a letting go—of the waking consciousness in the physical body. It would require courage to abandon ourselves, if we had to think about it. Of course this is not needed because we learned the knack before we were even born. So in this example, the second and third stages are lost in unconsciousness.

There is, however, a variant of sleep that displays all three steps and offers the closest analogy to entrance into the mystical state. This is out-of-body experience (see Chapter 12). In normal sleep we may be out of the body, but we seldom remember it. But it is possible to let go of the physical body and leap out into the astro-mental level with only a momentary break in consciousness. This happens spontaneously with some people, in response to great stress.

Though it is possible, it is unwise to attempt to induce separation deliberately. The experience will come of itself if and when one is ready for it. A barrier to it is fear of letting go of the familiar physical body. But conquering this fear does not of itself provide the means. Those who emerge into full consciousness out of the body usually report release (my third step) into a new and freer realm, devoid of the limitations of the physical body.

Of course, none of this *is* mystical experience. What, then, must we let go of to achieve this overwhelmingly greater experience? It is the entirety of our sense of selfhood that we must forego, not just the lower personal nature. In meditation it is possible to let go of this personal nature in steps, without any leaps. This situation can become habitual, leading to a stage when the spiritual nature is wholly in control in place of the personal nature. This condition has been called "transpersonal living," or "ego death." The lower nature, the ego of orthodox psychology, has "died," or rather has been superseded or relegated to the status of a servant to the higher nature.

However, this is still not a mystical state; something more has to be relinquished. If we return to our analogy of OBE, we can see what it is. In this lesser experience, we had to let go of the lowest element of the personality, namely the physical body. So by analogy, to achieve the mystical state, we must let go of the lowest element of the spiritual nature, and this is the abstract mind. We must transcend mentation in its entirety, because the mystical state lies wholly beyond mind as we have known it. A definite barrier has to be surmounted. We must purge ourselves of every vestige of selfhood or individuality before the mystical union can be attained. Then we shall face a miracle and a paradox, for we shall discover a new, more sublime kind of individuality.

It is not to be expected that the neophyte mystic should enter into the full potential of the mystical experience. There are far deeper experiences that may come when the state is established.

Once again, there are the three steps: letting go, the leap into the unknown, and the release into the bliss of the buddhic realm. There is an important difference, however, between OBE and mystical states. In the lesser out-of-body state we enter a realm that the personality is experienced in handling, that of thoughts and emotions. But although the spiritual individuality may be familiar with abstract thinking, it is quite unfamiliar with the buddhic realm. So the shock is greater, and the sense of release is also greater. St. Bonaventura wrote of the soul about to enter into this last state of contemplation: "There remains for it to transcend those things (every power of the human intellect) in contemplation, and to leave behind not only this world of sense, but also itself." And again, "That this transport may be perfect, it is necessary that all intellectual operations be abandoned within it." What holds us back from release is our habitual attachment to the personality with its multitude of likes and dislikes, and to our sense of self-identity, our regard for ourselves as persons of importance. All this possessiveness and attachment must be weakened greatly before we can hope to let go completely enough for even a brief glimpse of the Celestial City.

This prime necessity of letting go is emphasized by other mystics. Ken Wilber (1977) stresses that no Herculean feat of meditation or exotic yoga practice is required. Indeed no *positive* effort at all is needed, only this *negative* one of letting go. The operation is indeed negative, but that does not mean that it is passive. In this respect the analogy with sleep is imperfect; then we want only oblivion or pleasant dreams. When we are seeking the mystical state, passivity is replaced by a sense of eager expectation, a kind of intense focusing of consciousness. Yet, paradoxically, it must be done without effort or strain, but with quiet confidence that the miracle will be wrought in oneself, forthwith or when the time is ripe.

At the Star Camp in Ommen, Holland, in 1928, Krishnamurti made an impassioned plea to his listeners in his closing address. He begged them to realize that by simply letting go of all their beliefs and habits and listening closely to what he said, they could attain immediate liberation into a freer state. I can testify that his claim is indeed true. The trouble is that this state of grace does not persist, unless one is already well prepared. Old habits reassert themselves and the briefly enlightened one lapses back into fulfilling again the insistent demands of the personality. Yet all is not lost; his entire life henceforth may change gradually as a result of this brief event.

As is the case with intuition, it is not strictly speaking possible to *have* a mystical experience. While it persists "you" are transcended; "you" are not there at all, in any sense in which you normally regard yourself as you. Not only is the personal nature set aside but also (as I believe) the higher mind; total surrender is involved. Then whatever remains of "you" *becomes* the experience. There is a further analogy with the OBE in the duplicate world. Some subjects therein report looking down upon their own physical bodies as if at an external object of no special significance. So similarly from the mystical condition, it is sometimes possible to look "back" upon the entire personality, again regarding it as something of no special importance. It has its value and function, one perceives, but it is just one of many; it has no greater interest than the personalities of one's friends. Thus the mystical condition is not conducive to spiritual pride. While it lasts, there is nothing present that can feel such pride. In retrospect, the situation is recalled with wonder and humility.

THE VALUE OF MYSTICISM

Finally, the practical man may legitimately ask, "What is the value of mysticism anyhow?" It has indeed been suggested that mysticism is a luxury, that in evolutionary terms it has no survival value for the individual. That may seem to be true in the short term; in earlier centuries mysticism was often a route to martyrdom. Yet some of its martyrs have been canonized, and others are remembered as shining examples of mankind at its best. We know in our hearts that if we follow them we have a chance of creating some sort of Utopia on earth, but if we continue to give way to individual and national selfishness there is a real prospect of our civilization destroying itself in conflict. I believe, then, that mysticism is valuable for the very survival of the human race. Humanity is composed of individual human beings. Until a larger proportion of them learns to live in a truly human fashion, setting aside personal and sectarian interests for the good of the whole, this consummation cannot be. No government or institution, national or international, can be expected to work effectively until it is directed by such dedicated people. This is not religious piety, it is plain common sense.

MYSTICAL TRANSFORMATION

Another concept that may be helpful in trying to understand the nature of mystical experience is that of mystical transformation. In the long course of human evolution, our sense of individuality has come to rest at three highly distinct levels, but all three may be recapitulated in a single life. In worldly life, it comes to rest predominantly at the level of the personal nature, lodged in the physical body but ranging over emotional and lower mental levels. The spiritual nature then is expressed only through conscience and occasional altruism. At a later stage, some powerful stimulus brings about the first conversion, akin to the religious conversion of the born-again Christian. If this state persists, the sense of individuality is gradually transferred to the spiritual nature, operating at the higher mental level infused by intuition and selfless love. The personal nature is slowly transcended and relegated to a subsidiary status in which it is under control and no longer dominant.

Unfortunately, there is some possibility of confusing this lesser type of transformation with mystical transformation, for there are two stages of conversion. The first, religious conversion or the transfer of individuality from the personal nature to the spiritual nature, may well appear to the sudden convert as a transformation, and especially so if it is accompanied by premystical experiences; then it may easily be mistaken for the second conversion, the mystical transformation itself. There is no possibility of such an error if the subject has known any previous mystical experience. This "minor transformation" or first conversion is somewhat analogous to what Freud describes as "transformation from a pleasure ego to a reality ego." But the aspirant to mysticism must look to spiritual reality, not to the worldly counterfeit kind Freud had in mind. Another way of putting it is to say that when the first conversion becomes established, the subject gets into the habit of "looking to the Lord" when he meets any difficulty in his life. This helps him to shake off any "attachments" or "fixated deeds" (as the Upanishads describe).

Thus at a further stage in mystical experience, some people may undergo a second and more profound conversion. The purged and purified individuality, the human spirit, is raised up into its true realm and is joined to and merged into pure Spirit. Then the sense of individuality is almost extinguished in a mystical union with the Supreme, which is named in diverse ways as God, the Lord, the One, Brahman, the Source of Wisdom. Yet what remains is, paradoxically, intensified within the entire overwhelmingly glorious condition. It is now centered mainly in the divine nature, as it may be called, at the levels of atma and buddhi. This is the nature of the "I" that becomes the universe, in the lines from *The Light of Asia* quoted at the head of this chapter.

This then is the stupendous spiritual experience that has been named "mystical transformation" by a number of mystics. In this transformation the man is born again from above into a new world, a new way of life patterned on the Heavenly Man, so described by St. Paul; he becomes one with archetypal humanity. This is the consummation of spiritual love and wholeness. In this state of release from all conditioning, he knows Reality by direct understanding. His motivation is changed to willing obedience to the Source of all Wisdom. A new sense of responsibility changes his life for ever.

It should not be thought that the three seats of individuality are wholly exclusive. Consciousness is predominantly focused in one or another, but it can span adjacent pairs. Thus the spiritual nature participates to some degree in the mystical experience. Similarly, the mystical condition may endure with diminished intensity after return to a more normal level. Some echoes of that glory linger about him or her and may be discerned by others, sometimes even from a photograph. "Oh, what a lovely man," they may say, or, "He has the face of a saint." He can thereafter raise his consciousness to recapture that echo, not just as a memory, but its very nature. After repeated experiences like this, the transformation may become almost permanent and the mystical state habitual, relinquished only to concentrate on some mundane task.

RÉSUMÉ

The term "mysticism" has been debased in journalistic usage. It should be reserved for transcendental experiences of greater reality than psychic ones or the lesser ecstasies. Mystical consciousness is a somewhat rare state beyond intuition. Characteristics of both are contrasted. Examples of mystical experience, sometimes called

Cosmic Consciousness, are given. The nature of the experience is described, though its ineffability and intrinsic incommunicability make this difficult. It is nevertheless possible to study mysticism in a scientific manner. Criteria for the mystical state have been laid down, and have been quantified by scoring points for various characteristics, totalled as a General Index of Reality (GIR). This scheme also covers otherworldly experiences of lower grade. Mystical consciousness is achieved by grace rather than by effort. Nevertheless, preparations can be made, by way of spiritual living and meditation. Such experience should not be sought lightly and may prove unsettling for the ill-prepared. Contrary to some reports, psychedelic drugs do not induce a true mystical state. The analogies of learning to swim, going to sleep, and out-of-body experience are used to illustrate the knack of letting go that is involved. It is suggested that one must let go not only of the entire personality, but also of the higher mind. Strictly speaking "you" are simply not there at the time to "have" a mystical experience. Mysticism does have practical value. Practical mystics are the only people likely to lead the world out of its present confusions into some sort of Utopia.

In the course of transition from the worldly life to the spiritual and then to the mystical life, the sense of individuality becomes centered, in turn and mainly, at the levels of the personal, spiritual, and divine nature. The first transition is conversion, a minor transformation. The second is the major event known as mystical transformation. The experience involves consciousness at the buddhic level, by direct holistic identification and self-evident understandiing, in contrast to dualistic intellectual knowing.

Epilogue

The future is bound to surprise us, but we don't have to be dumbfounded.

Kenneth Boulding

Before considering future prospects, for individuals and for humanity, it is unhappily necessary to revert to the division made in Chapter 1 between materialists and others. By materialists I mean those who are, so to speak, mentally retarded by virtue of wilful refusal, despite all evidence, to admit the possibility of nonphysical life. If these materialists and reductionists sincerely maintain this stand, right up to the time of death, it seems possible that they will be granted the unfortunate satisfaction of being allowed to prove themselves right. They will deny themselves any conscious afterlife and will enter into the oblivion in which they believe.

The future that such individuals perceive for the human race is almost equally bleak. The most they can offer is ever-expanding technology, leading eventually perhaps to nineteenth century type colonialism, extending to the solar system and perhaps to our galaxy, using advanced spacecraft. The authors of a recent book, *The*

Anthropic Cosmological Principle (Barrow and Tippler 1986), expound authoritatively and at great length this principle, which affirms that the universe seems to have been almost designed to provide suitable conditions on Planet Earth, and possibly elsewhere, for a carbon-based biology leading to the evolution of man. However, they reject design and any Cosmic Intelligence. For them mankind's prospect, its "Omega Point," is domination over the galaxy. The possibility that human nature may itself evolve is hardly considered. Civilization will continue at the stage where avarice is in effect respected as a virtue. Better services will indeed be provided, but only secondarily; the primary objective will remain individual and corporate profits. World problems will be sorted out by means of the "technological fix." It is expected, despite much evidence to the contrary, that material prosperity will bring peace and happiness. For me, this is a grim prospect; if we persist in this path, then I believe civilization is more likely to destroy itself than to achieve Utopia.

PROSPECTS AS SEEN BY MYSTICS

But this is not the only path. Notwithstanding the misery, strife, and threats of war that now beset us, I believe that the true future of the human race is even now being disclosed by those who do admit, from faith or personal knowledge, that life *is* possible in nonphysical realms. I do not refer to sentimental attachment to the sensational aspects of psychism popular in some quarters, or in the half-hearted assent of churchgoers. I mean instead a strong faith supported by inner experience and conviction. A materialistic outlook, on the other hand, inhibits spiritual progress because Spirit is not even recognized. Faith makes it feasible, though by no means inevitable. It provides a rationale, and techniques are available; they are outlined in earlier chapters and in Chapters 15 and 16. Further cultural evolution is bound to include technological innovation, but this will be secondary. The primary advance will be concerned with the inner life, with the evolution of human nature itself. If the will is there, emotions and mind can be brought under control; the center of consciousness can be raised, at first sporadically, then permanently, to the levels of the spiritual nature. The apotheosis may come if this center is further lifted into the divine nature in mystical experience.

Moreover, mysticism is contagious, so to speak. Each mystic who describes his experiences vividly inspires many others to follow the same path. Thus, according to Peter Russell (1982), mystics proliferate exponentially. There may not be enough yet to have any great effect on the progress of civilization, but there soon will be. In the light of mystical understanding, problems resolve themselves. It becomes clear how to order one's life, and how to tackle the world's problems. Of course, everything cannot be put right overnight, nor even in centuries. But if one accepts this optimistic outlook, then *real* civilization will eventually be established, and the future of mankind on this planet be assured.

The possibilities for extraterrestrial civilizations may now be considered briefly. It is sheer geocentric arrogance to suppose that, out of the vastness of the universe, our speck of a planet is the exclusive haven for biological life. We may realize that this is so by considering how the most improbable ecological niches are richly colonized by chains of life forms. These range from the polar seas to hot springs and the thermal vents in the deep ocean floor, where sulphur substitutes for oxygen; also from cold dark caves to the searing heat of tropical deserts. This makes it highly probable that biological life forms exist on other planets, and possibly human civilizations. But belief in non-physical life opens up vastly the possibilities of intelligent life elsewhere in the universe. Even if Planet Earth is (improbably) unique in providing conditions for biological life, there could well be human civilizations living in superphysical realms, some of them more advanced than ours. If they had any interest in us, they would be more likely to visit in subtle bodies than in material spacecraft. If they wished to communicate, they would be less likely to use radio than to attempt telepathy. Conceivably, this is happening already; maybe our most sublime inspirations are extraterrestrial in origin.

PERSONAL SURVIVAL

Something more may be realized concerning personal survival. Can we realistically expect to pursue the theme of thinking beyond the portals of death? I suggest that we can. In Chapter 9 the case was argued that memory is not exclusively encoded in the brain; it is replicated at a nonphysical level of consciousness, namely in the mind. If this is accepted, then meaningful survival after the death of the physical body is at least feasible. There is also a good deal of evidence that survival does in fact happen. Many books—and novels—have been written on this topic. Just two recent ones may be cited that provide ample references for follow-up study. The first is my own *Our Last Adventure*. The other is the more closely argued and more fully documented *A Matter of Personal Survival* by Michael Marsh.

But what part of us is it that survives, and for how long? Such books as *The Tibetan Book of the Dead* and various theosophical writings suggest that after death the personal nature disintegrates as it is gradually transcended. Details of the earthly life that once occupied most of our attention slowly lose interest and pass from memory. Attention is transferred to a new way of living, still personal but little concerned with earth life. Then, at least with cultured or spiritually minded people, the center of consciousness becomes increasingly transferred from the personal to the transpersonal individuality, the spiritual nature. For many years, perhaps for centuries, insensitive to mortal time, we may bask in heavenly bliss, filled with noble thoughts. At long last, so we are assured, we get bored with all this ineffectual dreaming. Noble thoughts call for expression in action, and this can only be accomplished back on earth. Eventually then, our own volition coincides with what is inevitable in any event, and we are reborn to another earth life. Having discarded our memories of the former life, we are obliged to build up a new personality over the years. This is likely to display different aspects of our inner being, though doubtless there will be some resemblances to the former life. These notions may not be generally accepted in the West, but they do provide a logical scenario, and moreover tally broadly with the beliefs of at least half of the world's population.

Nevertheless, if a worldly person were to ask me if I believe in reincarnation, I should be tempted to answer, "No, what you regard as yourself will not reincarnate." It is the inner being, barely recognized through a worldly life, that returns. Thus we may say that the personality is immortal, though not everlasting, since it persists for a while after death. The individuality, the transpersonal spiritual nature, is everlasting though not eternal, since it persists through a long series of incarnations. Only the Spirit, the divine nature, of which we are as yet only dimly aware, is eternal. It abides quiescent in its timeless realm until we are ready to return to the Source whence we came, following in the footsteps of men like the Buddha and the Christ.

References

Bailey, A. A. 1956. *Telepathy and the etheric vehicle.* London: Lucas Press.

Barrow, J. D. and F. J. Tippler. 1986. *The anthropic cosmological principle.* Oxford: Clarendon Press.

Bohm, D. 1985. *Wholeness and the implicate order.* London: Routledge and Kegan Paul.

Brain-Mind Bulletin. (July 12, 1982; Oct. 3, 1983, and Dec. 30, 1985)

Bucke, R. 1961. *Cosmic consciousness.* New York: University Books.

Burden, V. 1987. *The process of intuition.* Wheaton, Ill.: Quest Books.

Castaneda, C. 1976. *Tales of power.* London: Penguin.

Chaudhuri, H. 1965. *Integral yoga.* London: George Allen and Unwin.

Davies, P. C. W., and J. R. Brown. 1986. *The ghost in the atom.* Oxford: Oxford University Press.

de Bono, E. B. (n.d.). *The use of lateral thinking.* London: Jonathan Cape.

———. 1985. *Masterthinkers handbook.* New York: International Center for Creative Thinking.

Denton, M. 1985. *Evolution: A theory in crisis.* London: Barnett Books.

Dewar, C. M., and R. Greenburg. 1969. *Nature* 223:183.

Dreyfus, H. L. and S. E. Dreyfus. 1986. *Mind over machine. The power of human intuition and expertise in the era of the computer.* London: Basil Blackwell Free Press.

Dunbar, R. 1984. *New Scientist* (Jan. 12): 26.

Earle, J. B. B. 1981. *Journal of Transpersonal Psychology.* Vol. 13, No. 2, p. 155.

Eccles, J. C., and D. N. Robinson. 1984. *The wonder of being human.* Boston: Shambhala.

——. 1980. *The human psyche.* Berlin, Heidelberg, New York: Springer-Verlag.

Evans, C. 1984. *Landscapes of the night: How and why we dream.* New York: Viking Press.

Ferry, G. 1987. *New Scientist* (July 16): 54.

Gardner, E. L. 1987 [1936, 1939]. *The play of consciousness in the web of the universe.* Wheaton, Ill.: Theosophical Publishing House. (Revised and combined edition of two books; orig. pub. London: Theosophical Publishing House.)

——. 1948. *The imperishable body.* London: Theosophical Publishing House.

Gilling, D., and R. Brightwell. 1962. *The human brain.* London: Orbis and BBC.

Goelet, P., and V. F. Castellucci, S. Schaber, and E. R. Kandel. 1986. *Nature* (July 31): 322.

Gooch, S. 1980. *New Scientist* (Sept. 11): 790.

Gray, W. 1982. Reported in *Brain-Mind Bulletin* (March 8 and 19, Sept. 13).

Green, A., and E. Green. 1978. *Beyond biofeedback.* New York: Delta Books.

Grey, M. 1985. *Return from death: An exploration of the near-death experience.* London: Arkana.

Hapgood, F. 1982. Computer chess bad—human chess worse. *New Scientist* (Dec. 23): 827.

Hearne, K. 1981. *New Scientist* (Sept. 24): 781.

Hinton, C. H. 1976 [1912]. *The fourth dimension.* Salem, N.H. Ayer; orig., London: George Allen.

Horne, J. 1982. *New Scientist* (Sept. 2, Nov. 12): 821, 429.

Jahn, R. G., and B. J. Dunne. 1986. *Frontiers of physics.* Vol. 16, No. 8 (Aug.): 721.

James, W. 1961. *The varieties of religious experience.* New York: Macmillan.

Karliss, M., and L. M. Andrews. 1973. *Biofeedback*. London: Garnstone Press.

Laski, M. 1961. *Ecstasy*. London: Cresset Press.

Marsh, M. 1985. *A matter of personal survival*. Wheaton, Ill.: Theosophical Publishing House.

Matthews, C., and J. Matthews. 1985, 1986. *The western way: 1. The native tradition; 2. The hermetic tradition*. London: Arkana.

Maxwell, N. 1987. *New Scientist* (May 14): 87.

Medawar, P. B. 1969. *Induction and intuition in scientific thought*. London: Methuen.

Mishkin, M., and T. Appelzeller. 1987. *Scientific American* (June): 62.

Mitchell, G. 1979. *Developing the mind with biofeedback*. London: Biofeedback Workshops.

Moody, R. A. 1976. *Life after life*. New York: Bantam. 1981. London: Mockingbird.

Morris et al. 1986. *Nature* (Feb. 27): 774.

Muldoon, S. J., and H. Carrington. 1963. *The projection of the astral body*. London: Rider.

Pahnke, W. 1969. in C. T. Tart. *Altered states of consciousness*. New York: Wiley.

Popper, K. R., and J. C. Eccles. 1977. *The self and its brain*. Berlin, Heidelberg, New York: Springer-Verlag.

Powell, A. E. 1969. *The etheric double*. Wheaton, Ill.: Quest Books. Orig. pub. London: Theosophical Publishing House.

Rendell, P. 1974. *Introduction to the chakras*. Wellingborough, Northants, England: Aquarian Press, p. 62.

Russell, P. 1982. *The awakening earth*. London: Routledge and Kegan Paul.

Silberstein, R. Private communication.

Slater, V. W. 1966. *Hatha yoga*. London: Theosophical Publishing House.

———. 1965. *Raja yoga*. London: Theosophical Publishing House.

Smith, A. 1984. *The mind*. London: Hodder and Stoughton.

Smith, E. L. 1986. *Our last adventure*. London: Theosophical Publishing House.

———, ed. 1975. *Intelligence came first*. Wheaton, Ill.: Theosophical Publishing House.

Taimni, I. K. 1975. *The science of yoga*. Wheaton, Ill.: Theosophical Publishing House.

Tweedie, I. 1979. *The chasm of fire*. London: Element Books.

Wallace, R. K., and H. Benson. 1972. *Scientific American* 220:85.

Whiteman, J. M. H. 1986. *The meaning of life*. Gerrards Cross, England: Colin Smythe.

———. 1961. *The mystical life*. London: Faber and Faber.

Wilber, K. 1978. *The atman project*. Wheaton, Ill.: Quest Books.

———. 1977. *The spectrum of consciousness*. Wheaton, Ill.: Quest Books.

Index

About the Author

E. Lester Smith, D.Sc., F.R.S., was elected a Fellow of the Royal Society in 1957 for research work in the vitamin field, especially for the isolation in 1948 of vitamin B_{12}. Receiving his Doctor of Science degree at the unusually early age of 28, he has authored approximately 100 research papers in numerous scientific journals, and has filed numerous patents. His book *Vitamin B_{12}* has been through three editions. During his illustrious career he has received several awards from scientific societies.

Dr. Smith is author of *Intelligence Came First, This Dynamic Universe,* and *Our Last Adventure,* all published by the Theosophical Publishing House.

Quest publishes books on Healing, Health and Diet, Occultism and Mysticism, Philosophy, Transpersonal Psychology, Reincarnation, Religion, The Theosophical Philosophy, Yoga and Meditation. **Other Quest Books on science and occultism include:**

Atoms, Snowflakes & God *by John L. Hitchcock*
A convergence of science and religion.

East Meets West: The Transpersonal Approach
Ed. Rosemarie Stewart. Examines the mind and "supermind."

A Human Heritage *by Alfred Taylor*
Integration of scientific data and human intuition.

Man, Visible and Invisible *by C.W. Leadbeater*
The colors in a person's aura. Color-illustrated.

A Spectrum of Consciousness *by Ken Wilber*
Synthesis of physics, religion, philosophy, psychology.

The Theatre of the Mind *by Henryk Skolimowski*
Evolution from instinct to intuition.

Thought Forms *by A. Besant & C.W. Leadbeater*
With 58 illustrations, many in color.

Thought Power *by Annie Besant*
Can our thoughts directly help or hurt others?

Two Faces of Time *by Lawrence Fagg*
Speculation about time based on physics and religion.

Available from:
The Theosophical Publishing House
306 West Geneva Road, Wheaton, Illinois 60187